Happy Easter to Sine
with love from Mommy
April 1974

The Year of the Badger

The Year of the Badger

by Molly Burkett

Illustrated by Pamela Johnson

J. B. LIPPINCOTT COMPANY • PHILADELPHIA AND NEW YORK

U.S. Library of Congress Cataloging in Publication Data

Burkett, Molly.
  The year of the badger.

  SUMMARY: A young English boy recounts his family's experiences
with a badger they raise from a sick baby.
  1. Badgers—Juvenile literature. [l. Badgers] I. Johnson, Pamela,
illus. II. Title.
QL795.B2B87 1974   639'.97'974443   73-19853
ISBN-0-397-31489-2

THIS BOOK IS DEDICATED TO THE CHILDREN,

ST. JOHN AND SOPHIE,

WHO WELCOME THE ANIMALS AND BIRDS INTO

THE FAMILY

AND MAKE THEM SUCH FUN TO HAVE.

1

MY NAME is St. John Burkett. I was born in Hampshire, England. At the time all this happened Mum and Dad and I and Sophie, who is my younger sister, were living in a village called Shalden. It is a little place perched on top of one of the rolling hills that make up the county. From anywhere in Shalden one can look down or across at more hills rolling away into the distance, covered with trees and fields. It is really deep in the country.

Mum and Dad ran an animal rehabilitation center in Shalden. It hadn't started as a center, but as a sort of hobby. The first year they kept count they had seven wild birds brought in, which they nursed and fed and eventually released. By the time I was born they were looking after about seventy birds a year, and Sophie and I cannot actually remember a time when we had fewer than about three hundred. Mostly birds came in, but we did have animals, too: deer and foxes and even stoats.

People got to know about the center, and we used to

go all around the country with Dad, collecting or releasing animals. Sophie and I used to moan a bit when we had to put off going to the pictures, or something like that, because of a sudden call for help with a swan that had got stranded or an owl stuck in somebody's chimney. Life was certainly never dull.

There are not many British birds that we have not had through the center at one time or another. Of course, most of them are pigeons and sparrows, but sometimes we get the rarer bird, like the hobby and the bittern, the kingfisher and the honey buzzard.

Nobody paid my parents for running the center. For a while Mum had a morning job, teaching, to pay for the animals' food and that sort of thing, but then the center got so busy this wasn't enough, and she started

8

running children's parties. I used to get my friends and organize concert groups for these. Sophie and her best friend, Julia, danced. They were quite good, really, except that they tended to argue all the time they were dancing. I did magic tricks, which were all right when they worked. Christine and Carol played recorders (they were really good), and David and Martin sang cowboy songs. These were very popular because everybody could join in, which was lucky, because often Martin would wait until the last minute and then go shy.

The idea of the rehabilitation center was to get sick animals and birds healthy enough to resume their life in the wild and then let them go. This is not always as easy as it sounds, for very often wild things do not want to go when they are well. They get used to having free meals and a lot of attention in the center.

Sometimes Dad had to refuse to accept an animal or bird because he knew it needed a vet's treatment and we could not afford it. He would give the people who brought it in the name of a good vet. But by the time a broken leg is X-rayed and set and the animal treated for infection it can cost a lot of money. There are not many people who are prepared to pay that kind of money in order to give an animal a chance to go back to the wild.

Sometimes people would want to pay us for looking after the birds and animals. Mum and Dad would not have this, because they felt if they started taking money they might begin to think of the money rather than the birds.

Nothing made Dad angrier than the people who came to our place and tried to put a price on the birds or animals. Quite often, when something was ready for release, somebody would offer to buy it. This was guaranteed to make Dad lose his temper.

"You can't put a price on wildlife!" he would shout, and I am sure the whole village could hear him. "Some things can't be measured in money."

Once he picked a man right off the ground and threw him out into the road. The man was going to start a zoo or something and just would not believe that our birds were not for sale.

Dad is right, though. You cannot put a price on freedom. And there is something really wonderful about seeing a bird that has come in sick and helpless finally fly away to its own world.

Not that it is always a success story. Some animals we could not help, and some seemed to lack the will to fight for their lives. Dad reckons that only about a third of the animals that come to us return successfully to the wild.

But Mum and Dad always make it quite clear when they take in a wild animal or bird that the aim is to release it to the wild eventually. They have to underline this, because sometimes we would get an animal into good condition, and then the people who had brought it in would try to demand it back again.

Sophie's friends seem to think Mum and Dad are a bit odd, having so many sick creatures around the house. My friends think it's super. They tell me how lucky I am. I suppose I am, really, but as I've never known a home that wasn't full of birds and animals of one sort or another, I cannot imagine any other kind.

I suppose it was not surprising that Nikki came to us in the first place.

2

IT WAS Sunday afternoon, and Tessa and I had been over the fields. Tessa was our dog, an English setter. She was everything that a dog should be, gentle and sweet with just that dash of independence and mischief that gave her character. She was beautiful and elegant, too.

We were back later than we meant to be. We had been taking the shortcut across Trinity Hill when Tessa stopped and pointed something. I looked in the direction she indicated but could not see anything. Whatever had caught her attention was so well camouflaged as to be almost invisible to the human eye.

Then I saw them: two young fox cubs. They were sitting at the bottom of the tumulus, an old burial mound, facing us, their eyes and ears alert. They must have heard us coming, for they sat as still as statues, staring in our direction, and their coloring blended perfectly with the tall wild grasses and young brambles.

Tessa and I remained stock-still, and suddenly, as if reassured, the cubs dashed at each other, both of them moving in the same instant. Over and over they rolled. Then, regaining their feet, they began to dash round and round and round in ever-tightening circles. Then up and down, up and down the length of the tumulus.

From where we stood, I could hear their sharp yaps and playful growls. They were like a couple of young puppies, except that in their play they were just that much more aggressive, more abandoned. Then the

larger of the two cubs sprang at its brother and knocked him flying. I had to laugh. I could not help it, the smaller cub looked so astonished.

Immediately the two young animals froze into immobility, alert and cautious, staring fixedly in our direction. Then they resumed their play, moving in unison as if they were practicing some kind of telepathy.

I could have watched them for hours, but Mum is never very pleased when I am late for Sunday tea, so we continued on our way across the ten-acre field.

Then Tessa spotted a hare and was after it like a shot. There seems to be something about rabbits that really arouses the hunting instinct in a dog, and Tessa was no exception. I called her to heel immediately, but she took not the blindest bit of notice and continued the chase, giving cry like a hound. I was furious. I was not worried about the hare; I knew she would never catch that in a month of Sundays. From where I stood I could see it maneuvering itself into a favorable position to make a good run uphill and use its long back legs to its best advantage.

It was Tessa's refusal to come to heel that made me angry with her. In the country a disobedient dog cannot be tolerated, especially if there are sheep or the landowner has pheasants.

I had to chase her all the way back, right up the path by which we had come, and give her a well-deserved slap while she was still being disobedient. She knew she had done wrong, and as I reached her she lay down on the ground and gazed up at me with large reproachful eyes. I nearly gave way, but I knew that would be no good. She had to learn to do as she was told. I gave her one short sharp slap and told her she was a bad dog.

She looked at me in such a way that I could imagine her trying to say she was sorry. She could not have stayed closer to me after that, all the way home.

I heard a noise as we turned in at the gate. It surprised me so that I stopped in my tracks and listened. It was a baby. There was no mistaking that noise, and it was coming from our house.

I crept into the living room. There were Mum and Dad and Sophie, all engrossed with something in a box by the fire. Nobody noticed that I was a bit late home or that my Sunday trousers had got rather dirty.

I sidled up and looked in the box myself. No wonder everyone was too preoccupied to notice me. The tiniest, most pathetic little creature was lying there. It was a young badger, so small that it couldn't have been more than about six weeks old. It lay on its side, a miserable little thing barely eight inches long, with black and white guard hairs sparsely covering its pink body. It was caked all over with dried mud. Its muzzle was blunt and pink and soft, showing that it was still relying on its mother's milk for food.

We had had badgers before, but never one as small and sick as this one. You could see that it was very, very ill. It lay on some straw at the bottom of the box, and despite the warmth of the fire, it shivered ceaselessly. It made a weak continuous crying that sounded just like a very young human baby.

"It's not fair to keep it alive," said Dad compassionately.

To our surprise, Mum turned on him. She does not often lose her temper, but she did that day.

"People who say things like that," she stormed, "make me sick. They never think what is the proper thing to do. Oh, no, just what is the easiest for them. This little thing has had a rotten deal. It deserves a chance at life, and the least we can do is give it that chance."

"I'll warm some milk," I offered, trying to calm her down.

"Cow's milk by itself will be far too strong," Dad said. He was obviously willing to go along with Mum if she felt so strongly about it. "I should think we'd be safe on a fifty-fifty mixture, milk and boiled water, but how we'll get it down the little animal I don't know."

"What about my doll's bottle?" Sophie suggested, and she was off to fetch it before Dad could answer. It was not such a bad idea, either. The teat on that small bottle would be much easier to get into the young badger's mouth than a teaspoon or something like that.

She was back with it before I had the milk ready. It took some patience to get the milk into the bottle, but nothing like as much as Mum needed when she tried to get it into the badger.

Holding the animal in her lap, she eased the teat gently into its mouth and squeezed the bottle, but the baby badger made no attempt to swallow. The warm liquid spilled out of the side of its mouth and over Mum's hands and skirt. Then she tried dipping her fingers in the warm milk and putting them in the badger's mouth.

"The poor thing's too weak to suck," she said.

She must have got something down it, though, because the little animal stopped crying and fell into an uneasy sleep. A short while later it was crying again, and we went through the whole feeding exercise once more. Mum was frightened that we would give it too much, since it had obviously had no nourishment at all for some time, but there wasn't much danger of that. The badger would take only four or five drops and then it would fall asleep.

"It's all we can do," said Dad. "Give it food and warmth. The rest is up to the badger."

The badger seemed to appreciate this itself. Every time it woke, Mum would give it a little nourishment. When she put her finger with the warm milk on it into the animal's mouth, she said it was making an effort to swallow, although we could see no movement in the throat. It fell into a more settled sleep, too, although every so often it would cry out with such intensity that it startled itself awake. It would look mistrustingly round and then settle down to sleep until it startled itself awake again. I reckoned it was dreaming and wondered what such a tiny animal could have to dream about and what had caused it to be in such a dreadful state.

We had to wake it up to give it its eight o'clock feeding. We had decided hourly feedings were too frequent, and we thought we would try to start it on a two-hour schedule and lengthen it to three hours as soon as possible.

The badger would not settle down after that eight o'clock feeding. It whimpered and wriggled like a spoiled child. Sophie was getting ready for bed, stretching out the process as long as she could. She was half in and half out of her nightgown when she said casually, "I reckon it wants to go to the toilet."

We had not thought of this. The badger had taken a lot of liquid by now and seemed quite pot-bellied. I took it out into the garden. It relieved itself immediately, and when I put it back in its box it settled down with a contented little grunt.

Of course, that quite won Mum's heart. To think that, as sick as it was, the little animal would not soil its own box.

I looked at it before I went up to bed. It still looked horribly weak and ill and pathetically small.

I did not rate its chances high.

3

THE NEXT MORNING I made a beeline for the box as soon as I came downstairs. I tried to convince myself that the badger was looking just a little livelier, that its eyes were a little brighter, that it was able to hold its head up just a little.

But that was wishful thinking. The animal was the same as it had been the previous evening. There was the same labored breathing, the same tacky coat, the same pathetic, humanlike whimpering. As I gazed at its tiny black and white form, all I could really tell myself was that at least it was no worse.

I went off to school reluctantly. I knew there was nothing I could do, but I hated leaving it alone in the house. Mum would be home at lunchtime—this was when she was teaching in the mornings—and she was going to try to get home at recess to give it a mid-morning feeding.

If it had been stronger, she would have taken it with her. She often used to fill the car with fledglings and pop out between classes to push some food down their throats. The longest you can leave a young bird without food is two hours, and tiny birds like wrens and bluetits need to be fed even more frequently. Most summers we used to drive round with the alarm clock set to remind Mum when it was time for something or other to be fed. Sophie and I got used to having to fetch Mum out of some shop or other to tell her that the alarm clock had gone off. We got some funny looks sometimes. But the badger was different. It needed warmth and quiet as much as anything else.

I skipped a football practice to get home early that day. When we got to our gate, I lost courage and asked Sophie to go first to see if the badger was still alive. She need not have bothered. As soon as she opened the door we could hear it crying.

Mum was getting its food ready. She had had two calls out that afternoon and was a bit upset about the second one. Some boys had been keeping an owl that they did not know what to feed or how to keep clean. When they realized it was sick, they had started feeding it on yeast. When Mum got there, the poor thing was blown up like a balloon. She was horrified that the boys' parents had allowed the bird to get in such a state before they sought help.

On the trip out she had found a store that had a fountain pen filler in stock. This is a long slender glass tube with a very small opening at one end and a rubber bulb at the other. She was filling it up with the milk and water solution and testing it. The liquid came out in a small powerful jet, every bit as strong as my old water pistol.

"I'll have to squeeze the bulb slowly," Mum said. "It won't do the badger any good to have milk shot down its throat at that speed."

But the little animal was not having any of it. As Mum eased the filler into the side of the badger's mouth, it would turn its head and the milk would dribble down its chest. As weak as it was, it had the strength to resist that fountain pen filler and try Mum's patience in no uncertain terms. Then, finally, she got the end of the tube into the side of its mouth and triumphantly squeezed the rubber bulb.

I thought she had killed it.

She must have forgotten about the force of the jet, and she had emptied the lot down the badger's throat in one go. The poor little thing coughed and spluttered. Liquid dribbled from the side of its mouth and from its nostrils. Then it shuddered. Its head dropped onto Mum's lap, and it lay still. I thought it was breathing its last, and so did Mum. Gently she laid it in its box. It just lay there with its eyes shut, its sides heaving, while we watched miserably.

Then with a shake of its head it looked up and around at our worried faces, as if to say, "That had you all worried," and started to weep again.

Mum refused to go on with the fountain pen filler, so I said I would try. I knew I had to get the milk

gradually into the badger's mouth so that it would swallow naturally. If the milk went into its throat too quickly, there was danger of its going down the wrong way and into the lungs and drowning the little thing.

I soon found it easier said than done. The badger would not have that tube in its mouth. It would wait until I had the milk easing nicely from the end of the filler, and just at the inopportune moment, it would move its head, not much, just a fraction of an inch, but enough to make sure that I was squirting the warm liquid over my school trousers instead of down the badger's gullet.

"It's this glass thing," I said. "The badger doesn't like it in its mouth."

"Well, glass must be a bit foreign to it," said Mum. "I wonder if it would take it if we put some valve rubber on the end."

That was something we had in plenty. I was always getting punctures in my bike tires, and I had two or three patch kits in my bedroom. We had soon fitted a short length onto the end of the filler.

But the badger had no intention of having anything to do with this either, and I went through the same antics of pouring milk over my trousers instead of down the animal's throat. It was not long, though, before I could anticipate its next move, and as it moved its head, I would move the filler in the same direction. Then, when I considered it safe, I squeezed the rubber bulb gently and two or three drops of warm liquid trickled into its mouth.

The badger swallowed. It was an automatic movement, I know, but the badger made no attempt to reject the food, and from that moment feeding ceased to be a worry. It still objected to the fountain pen filler and continued to fight against the valve rubber, but as soon as one of us managed to ease the tube into its mouth, it accepted it. By the end of the week the badger would start to suck as soon as it was in.

I gave the badger three fillers full that first feeding. It was a long and tedious job, easing the liquid into its mouth a few drops at a time, but the filler held the equivalent of two teaspoonfuls, so the animal didn't do too badly. It would have taken more, but Mum intervened.

"Never force an empty stomach," she said. "You'll do more harm than good."

The badger seemed to accept our mixture of cow's milk and water. At first we kept to the fifty-fifty mixture, but we soon made it a little stronger, six parts of milk to four parts of water. We added glucose and calcium gluconate to give extra nutrition. Later we fed the badger some general vitamin extracts that the vet gave us, but we knew that initially calcium was vital, as it is for all animals reared in captivity.

I shall never forget Mum bringing the calcium tablets out from her bag. She had been down to town especially to get them and was pleased with herself for remembering. Each tablet was over half an inch in diameter, bigger in fact than the little badger's paws. Sophie just stood there and giggled.

"However are you going to get one of those down the poor thing?" Dad asked.

Mum obviously had not thought about that. "I'll mash them up," she said confidently.

Those tablets were as hard as nuts. When she pressed on them, trying to crush them, they shot across the room like bullets. No amount of banging, soaking, or crushing would break them up fine enough to go into the milk.

Sophie's giggles got so bad she had to go into the living room to sit down and recover.

The next day Mum went down to town and got calcium in powder form. The tablets are still in the larder, probably waiting for an orphaned elephant.

4

THE LITTLE BADGER hovered between life and death for three days and nights. Each night when we went to bed, each morning when we left for school, we wondered if it would pull through. And each time I looked into its box and saw that it was still breathing seemed like a miracle.

Its life followed the same pattern day and night. Mum said that it was as bad as having a real baby. It was fed every three hours, and after each feeding it was put on a patch of earth where it made its mess. It never once soiled its box, although it was so ill. Then it was put back in the box in the warm and just slept until its next feeding.

When I came home from school that third day, I went straight in to look in the box. The little animal lifted its head right off the cloth in its box and looked up at me. It was the first time that it had the strength to do it.

"Hello, little fellow," I said. And just as if it understood what I had said and what had been happening to it, it nickered back at me.

There is no other word to describe the noise it made. In a way it seemed little more than the noise it had been making all along, but I knew it was different. I was quite sure that it was a little noise of recognition and welcome.

I picked the tiny creature up and held it in my hands. It pressed its little cold nose against my wrist and gave a sigh that sent a shiver through its whole body. It was the most endearing little bundle of fur

that you could imagine. The fact that it was so sick just seemed to make it more precious.

I gently turned it over, for we had wondered whether it was male or female. It was a female. I knew she had to be handled very carefully, so I just sat with her on my lap, fondling her gently behind her ear, easing out the flakes of dried mud. She seemed to enjoy it, shutting her eyes and giving a long-drawn-out grunt.

Dad was surprised when he came home from work and saw the badger. "I wouldn't have believed it possible," he said. "I don't mind admitting now I didn't think we had a chance of pulling her through. I would have been much happier if we had had her put to sleep. But she's over the hump now. I think she's going to get better."

Sophie was holding the badger then. She was sitting up in Sophie's arms and looking round at everyone, her head cocked a little to one side. She was still weak, still tiny, but no longer was she just a sick baby animal. Suddenly she had become a young badger.

Sophie was making a fuss of her, sitting there stroking and kissing her. Then she put the animal down on the floor and said, "There you are, badger. You have a walk round while I tidy up your box."

The badger sat half on her side, looking up at us. Then she moved toward Mum and we all stood and watched, completely horror-struck.

I say "moved" because you could never have said she walked. She moved her forelegs correctly enough, but her back legs trailed behind her, stiff and useless. She dragged them after her like a piece of putty. Her hindquarters were completely paralyzed.

I cannot say how long we stood there watching, unable to move or utter a sound. Sophie began to cry. I knew how she felt. I could have cried myself. Just when we thought we had won, that the badger was going to get better—this.

I have never seen anything more pathetic. The young animal dragged herself right across to Mum. She sat on Mum's feet and looked up at her, nickering in just the same way that she had to me earlier on. Mum stared at her. For a minute I thought she was going to cry, too.

It was Dad who broke the silence. "We should have known there was something wrong with it. Badgers are good parents. They would never have deserted this little thing if there had been nothing wrong with it."

"We still may be able to save it," Mother said defiantly. "I'm going to phone the vet first thing in the morning. There must be something we can do."

She bent down and picked up the badger and put her gently back in her box. When I went up to bed that evening I felt really miserable.

I was a bit late waking up the next morning. Dad had already gone to work, and Mum was sitting near the fire with the badger on her lap and a bowl of warm water and disinfectant beside her.

"I've phoned the vet," she said. "He'll be up in half an hour. I'm just getting the badger a bit clean for his visit. It's about time I washed some of this mud off."

The badger had been so weak that we had decided not to bother about cleaning her up properly until she was stronger. She looked much better now. Her little head was erect, and she turned toward each of us when we spoke as if she were really joining in the conversation.

Sophie and I had just started our breakfast when Mum's startled "Oh!" made us look in her direction.

"What's the matter?" Sophie asked.

"This isn't mud at all. Look!" said Mum.

We went over. Mum had been cleaning up one of the animal's ears. She had eased off the first piece of what we had thought was mud, and she was right. It was not dirt; it was a great ugly scab that had come away, revealing a huge gaping sore, so deep that it was a wonder it hadn't penetrated to the brain.

I took the animal from her and gently washed some more dirt away. It was another scab, revealing another ugly sore. The little badger was covered with them; at least a third of her body must have been eaten into.

"I don't think we should do any more," Mum said dispiritedly. "We'll wait for the vet. He won't be long now."

He had not arrived by the time I had to leave for school. He passed me halfway down the lane. He slowed right down and leaned out to speak to me, but

I rushed past the car. I did not want to speak to anyone just then, especially not the vet. The little badger was in such a pitiful state that I was sure the vet would advise Mum to have her destroyed.

I could not concentrate on anything at school that day. My mind was filled with the picture of that poor young badger and those useless hind legs and filthy gaping sores. It all seemed so hopeless.

5

I HUNG ON at school until late that evening and missed the school bus. Generally I went on the bus because we lived four miles out of town, but I sometimes missed it in the mornings and had to get my bike out. At that, I could usually beat the bus to school by the time it had wound round the hamlets and villages collecting other country children.

This time I had to walk, and when I got home I had to make a conscious effort to go through the gate. We had only had the badger for a few days, but in that short time she had really become part of the family.

Sophie was getting the tea. She is quite good at that sort of thing, although she turns a loaf of bread into the most peculiar shape. It was not the tea table that attracted my attention, though. It was the brown cardboard box near the stove. It was still there.

Then the badger was still alive? I hardly dared to look. But from the bottom of the box the small black and white face lifted, two tiny dark eyes looked in my direction, and the little badger gave the same nicker of recognition with which she had greeted me the previous day.

Mum came in just then. "The vet says she's going to be all right," she said happily. "He thinks she will lose her tail, and her coat will be a bit patchy for some time, but what does a tail matter? She's going to pull through, and that's what really counts. He's giving her penicillin to get rid of the infection, and he thinks the paralysis will wear off by degrees. He's going to look in again tomorrow. Do you know, I could have kissed him when he said that she was going to get better."

I knew how she felt. Suddenly I felt on top of the world, too. I found I was starving and wolfed down the tea Sophie had prepared.

Afterward, Tessa and I went over the fields, and I sang the whole way. Everything felt right with the world. Down in the fold in the hills I could see Mr. Dodds, the shepherd, and the young lambs skipping and gambolling around without a care. Out across the field three hares were chasing round and round in ever-tightening circles until they were almost on top of one another. Then two of them stood up on their hind legs and began to lunge at each other while the doe sat quietly watching until she tired of them and wandered off to the edge of the field, where she started to nibble the coarse winter grass.

Tessa had seen the hares, too, and would have given chase, but I sensed what she had in mind and forbade

her to move. I could see her hesitate, wondering
whether she would risk it or not, and then deciding
she had better do as she was told. She sat back, put her
chin down on her chest, and lookeed up at me coyly
with her dark gentle eyes.

We found an early lapwing's nest in the young wheat
and I wondered about taking the two eggs back to Dad.
He used to enjoy them for breakfast. Lots of people
think them a great delicacy, and lapwing eggs are not
protected until April 15, because eggs laid before that

date rarely hatch. However, I did not think it was fair to interfere with them, so I left them there.

We cut back into the lane and met Sophie, trying to balance on her new two-wheeler. She wobbled along home with us. When we got in, Mum was sitting by the fire with the badger in her lap and poking at her with the eyebrow tweezers.

She was so involved with what she was doing that she did not notice Sophie and me.

"Whatever are you doing, Mum?" Sophie asked.

"I've got to get these ticks off," she replied, probing with the tweezers.

"Have you got to get them out like that?" Sophie said, horrified. "Why can't you just pull them off?"

"You can't do that," Mum told her. "You've got to get the heads out, you see. Ticks live by sucking blood, and they bury their heads beneath their victim's skin. If you pull them off, you will probably leave their heads inside the body, and then you really can have trouble, because the places swell up and fester. I've loosened their hold with paraffin, so they're not too bad to get off. Look at that one there, do you see the way its body is blown up? It's swollen with the poor little badger's blood."

She eased the insect off and put it on a piece of newspaper.

The thought of those repulsive insects really sickens me. As I write this I can feel detached, yet I know one glimpse of the tiny parasites would fill me with the same kind of revulsion I felt when I realized the extent of the damage they were causing to the little badger.

At first sight ticks seem harmless enough—small, black, and shiny—but they attach themselves to their host with limpetlike tenacity and refuse to loosen their hold until they are fat and bloated with blood. Only then will they let go and drop off.

A healthy animal may pick up an occasional tick from long grass, but never in quantity, and the tick will not get the chance to reattach itself, once it has dropped off, because the animal is moving about. But a sick animal cannot get away and must tolerate reinfestation time after time. As the ticks suck, they weaken an already weak creature, and from the moment they attach themselves to the poor animal they cause distress. If the animal manages to get the tick off, as often as not the forepart is left inside the host's body and continues the malignant work by injecting poison into the system and causing an infection.

This was the difficult part of cleaning the badger: getting those horrible ticks off without leaving the heads behind to wreak further damage. Mum had wiped her all over with paraffin, and some of the ticks did loosen their hold, but the rest we had to prise off. A long, unenjoyable, and seemingly never-ending task it was. There always seemed to be more that we hadn't noticed. They would swell up to three or four times their normal size before we spotted them.

Mum did most of the work. She pulled them off with

her eyebrow tweezers, one by one. None of us could bear to touch the insects with our fingers. Sometimes Mum would hold the tweezers too tightly. The insect would burst like a miniature paper bag, and the reddish-brown liquid that I knew was the little badger's life blood would squirt out.

We have grown more experienced in our treatment of ticks now. We rub the poor victim down with a strong wash which we get from the vet. This loosens the hold of most of the ticks, and only the most tenacious have to be prised off.

I remember a ferret being brought in one day, which had been picked up in a parking lot in the middle of a town. It was so covered with ticks that it looked as though it was wearing a necklace. Another victim was a large bird that had been picked up by a courting couple in the New Forest. Dad could not identify it immediately, but when the young couple had gone he had a good look at it. Imagine his consternation on realizing that what he had thought were black rims round the eyes were layers of ticks, many of them attached firmly round the eyelids and some of them with their heads actually buried inside the rims. That was a difficult job, because we were afraid to use the wash or paraffin or anything round the bird's eyes. We never did completely get rid of those ticks, until the bird itself was fit again and ready to go and had revealed itself as a very ordinary common buzzard.

6

THE VET CAME UP the following Saturday and gave the badger her final penicillin injection. He also took off the last of the detested ticks. He was much more efficient about it, touching each bloated insect with a lighted cigarette. That made them contract instantly, and he just pulled them off.

"There you are," he said as he stood up, "that's all we can do for the little lady. It's just a matter of time now."

"What about her back legs, though?" Mum asked.

"They will get stronger as the infection recedes," he said confidently. "She'll be all right."

The badger did get stronger. At first her improvement was so gradual that we, who were living with her, failed to see it. She just slept and ate. Day after day she followed the same monotonous routine.

Then the miracle happened.

I put her on the floor one day so that I could clean up her box, and she *walked*. I suppose most people would have called it a shuffle. We would not have cared what you called it. She had actually moved her back legs. She was going to get better. We all stopped what we were doing and watched her as she belly-crawled across the room, all four legs moving spasmodically. Up to that moment I think we had all secretly doubted that she would ever really be able to walk or lead a natural life.

It was six weeks before those great gaping sores finally healed, and another two weeks before her legs were strong enough for her to run about normally. But we had started with a weak, sick, pathetic little animal, and we now had a happy, affectionate, boisterous, half-grown badger.

She had not developed her badger characteristics suddenly. She had been growing and changing so steadily that we hardly noticed the change, until one day, there she was—and we had Nikki.

Sophie thought of the name. "It sounds as if she says 'Nikki, nikki, nikki,' when she runs to meet us, so that's what I'm going to call her," she announced one day.

So Nikki she was. The badger seemed to understand immediately. She would look up the minute we called her name and often replied with a "Nikki, nikki, nikki" of her own. The two sounds were really very similar. Perhaps she thought we were trying to imitate a badger and was giving us a little encouragement.

By this time it was the middle of May and we had had Nikki for two months. May is the time when Mum and Dad start their busiest season with the birds, and the whole family has to help. Dad reckons that over the year we average about six birds a week, of which we get about a third away eventually. That year we were having five a day as well as an occasional animal. Some of the birds that came in were difficult ones that needed a lot of attention. We had a cuckoo that had been picked up with pneumonia, a green woodpecker that had been knocked over, a honey buzzard that had been picked up in Cornwall with a broken wing. Mum and Dad were so busy one night that they did not have time to go to bed at all.

My job was to look after Nikki.

It was difficult to remember her as the weak little bundle she had been when she was first brought to us. I certainly had no trouble feeding her now. When we saw her tucking into her meals with such enthusiasm, it was hard to believe there had been a time when it was almost impossible to get a single drop of milk down her gullet. Mealtimes nowadays were a different matter! She had the same food as Tessa. Leastways, that was the idea, but Nikki was prepared to sample anything edible. If the family were passing round cookies or chocolates, Nikki would dash from one to the other of us in an absolute frenzy in case she was going to be left out. She would nicker with sheer delight if she discovered an old candy wrapper or a discarded sandwich.

We fed Nikki and Tessa together. I often wished I

could draw, for the two animals made such a delightful picture: two black and white heads eating busily
from the same bowl. We had to stop doing this quite
soon, though. Food rapidly became the mainspring of
Nikki's life. To have to share any of it with Tessa was
more than she could bear. Mealtimes became a race,
the idea being to see which of them could get most
down her throat in the shortest time.

Nikki hit on a fine solution, whether by intelligence
or pure accident I never determined. Whatever the
reason, the results were certainly effective. When I put
food down for the animals, Nikki promptly *sat in the*

dish. She could contort herself so that she could bend down and fish out the choicest bits of meat from underneath her tubby form, while poor Tessa was prancing round unable even to get a look in. By the time we went to find out why Tessa was barking so frantically, there would generally only be the dog meal and gravy left.

Obviously, we had to give them different dishes, but this was not really the answer, because Nikki would dash from one to the other of them like a horizontal yo-yo until she got herself in such a state that she had hiccups. In the end we had to feed them in different rooms, just to make sure that Tessa got a well-balanced meal. Nikki, being that much shorter in the leg, quite literally had a head start and was able to sneak out the pieces of meat from beneath Tessa's nose.

Nikki was always regretful at the end of a meal. She would nose all round the plate, even tip it upside down in case some edible pieces had worked their way underneath. She would try to lick the pattern from the plate. When she was sure that there was not another morsel left, she would amble over to her favorite easy-chair in the corner of the living room and clamber up into it. With a great reverberating sigh she would sink back against the cushion and nod off to sleep, exposing her little round tummy, her forepaws crossed loosely over it and her head lolling gently to one side. Every so often her body would be shaken by a deep, exaggerated sigh, sometimes so loud that it would startle her awake.

On these occasions she would look round accusingly at everyone in the room. Then, with a disgruntled grunt, she would relax and resume her after-dinner nap.

We never fed Nikki raw meat, although we knew it would be a more natural diet for her than the cooked variety. We wanted to dull the killing instinct in her and thought that there was a chance that she would come to associate red meat with living animals. We knew that it was unlikely that she would set out to kill. Badgers live mainly on roots and insects in the wild, although you do sometimes find a rogue badger, one that will search out chickens or sitting pheasants and kill them. These are generally old badgers whose teeth have worn down so much that they find it difficult to get enough to eat through foraging. I will not say that a badger won't take a chicken or a rabbit if it comes on one in its wanderings, but badgers will not deliberately set out to hunt, the way foxes do. All the same, the instinct to kill is there, and we did not want to encourage it in Nikki. With sick and injured wild birds on the premises, she could have become a menace.

We took her pacific nature very much for granted. Looking back, I realize that now. She shared the garden with many other wild things, yet she never attempted to touch or threaten even the smallest bird, not even the old Khaki Campbell duck which somebody had picked up in the middle of the highway and which had taken over the premises as soon as it left its basket. It would waddle around all day, talking away to itself, objecting vociferously if anything stepped out of line, Nikki included, and the badger accepted it with the same aplomb as she did everything else.

However, the day came when Nikki began to make her presence known at our mealtimes. It was my fault to begin with, because when she was really small I had allowed her to stay on my lap during meals. Now I was paying for it. As soon as we sat down for a meal, Nikki would go frantic, scrabbling up to try to get onto the table, clambering onto my lap, bristling with enthusiasm and determination to get her own way. Of course, in no time at all she was going a bit further and trying to help herself to the food on the table.

Sophie was the trouble then. As soon as Nikki started her antics, Sophie would start to giggle. All she could see from her side of the table was that little handlike paw creeping surreptitiously over the table edge, or a little black button of a nose worming itself steadily above the table top. The day that Nikki took the wrong path and suddenly appeared out of the top of my sweater was nearly too much for Sophie. She laughed so hard she had to leave the table.

That excited Nikki, too. She dashed around the table like a thing possessed, tripping over everyone's feet, showing off in real badger style. It's very difficult to discipline a lively badger when you have a sister who will not be serious.

When Nikki started the same tactics at our evening meal, it became too much of a good thing. Obviously it was impossible to expect her to practice any kind of self-control when there was food around. I was making no headway at all with her training, so, for our own peace of mind and Sophie's digestive system, we put Nikki in her box in the kitchen when we were eating. Not that this actually gave us much peace. Our meals were accompanied by the noise of a very bad-tempered badger, nickering and grunting with her nose pressed firmly to the gap beneath the door.

7

TESSA HAD a lot to put up with from Nikki, yet she was touchingly patient with her, especially at the beginning when the badger was very small. She seemed as delighted as we were when Nikki really began to get well, and encouraged the young animal in her first steps by constantly nosing her beneath her stumpy little tail. Nikki had not lost her tail as the vet had expected. It looked a little moth-eaten where the hair had come out, but that was all. Sometimes Tessa would be a little too zealous and would give an over-helpful shove that would tip Nikki head over heels, but the badger bore the setter no ill will. When Nikki really began to walk properly, Tessa would bow right down on her front legs, wagging her tail and barking encouragement.

It seemed no time at all before Nikki was strong enough to enjoy a game with Tessa. I bought her a rubber bone and a ball, thinking she would play with them like a young pup. She did nose them around for a couple of minutes, but was soon bored and discarded them. She preferred to play with Tessa.

She could not bear for the dog to be sleeping when she wanted to play. She would stalk up softly to Tessa's tail, tweak a hair on it, and jump backward as though expecting some action from the recumbent dog. Or she would go round to the other end and press her little black button of a nose against Tessa's nose and sigh deeply. If that did not rouse Tessa, the badger would bounce all around the dog with much the same rhythm as a bouncing ball, all four feet off the ground at the same time, nickering continuously until, in the end, Tessa would resignedly give up sleeping, get to her feet, and start to play. She would pat Nikki gently with her forepaw or amble gently round the table with the badger bouncing along happily behind her. Nikki would soon grow tired, though, and the two animals would sink down in front of the fire together. They made a lovely picture, two black and white animals curled round carefully in a semicircle with Nikki tucked inside. They looked just like a living hearth-rug.

The whole family loved Nikki, but she was really my particular pet. It isn't true to say that she followed me around like a dog, because she kept even closer than that. She would follow so hard on my heels that it was difficult not to kick her at every step. Tessa had to take second place to the assertive badger but would walk as close as possible behind the rumbustious little animal, so we presented quite a little procession when we went out for a walk, especially if the swan or the old Khaki Campbell duck joined on behind. Neither of these last two had much stamina, though, and both generally gave up before we reached the first corner.

At first Nikki had to be carried a good deal of the way, and although she was still quite small, barely eighteen inches long, she was exceptionally heavy for her size and must have weighed well over fifteen pounds. My arms used to ache by the time we reached home. There was no chance of leaving her behind, though. As soon as Tessa and I prepared to go out, Nikki was at my heel, shadowing my every movement so closely that you would have thought she had been glued to me.

When we set out, she would be full of enthusiasm, bouncing along behind me. Then, suddenly, without warning, she would have had enough. Realizing I no longer had a small animal virtually attached to me, I would look back, and there would be Nikki, stretched out on the ground, four legs splayed out, dead to the world.

That was the end of the "walk" part. I carried her the rest of the way. Sometimes she would regain enough energy to take a little more exercise, but it would soon be terminated by the same sudden total collapse.

Another habit that Nikki developed at a very early age, and which became very pronounced as her legs strengthened and she moved about more, was the business of squatting. If a stranger came into the room, if she was disturbed by an unusual noise or upset in any way, she would run to the nearest familiar object and squat on it, leaving a drop of liquid behind. As her favorite spot soon came to be my feet, I became quite used to it. She did it so often that my school shoes had a permanently bleached spot on the toes where Nikki had left her mark.

Every day when I came home from school she would run and squat on my shoe. Sometimes she did it if I had been out of the room for only five minutes. The rest of the family suffered similar treatment, though nothing like as often. Mum nearly had a fit the first time Nikki did it to her. She thought the badger was making a mess on her shoe.

The drop of liquid a badger deposits when it squats leaves a faint musty smell, because it comes from the scent gland beneath the animal's tail. I have been told that badgers developed this habit as a means of recognizing certain objects again. Badgers are notoriously shortsighted, but they have an extremely strong sense of smell. They can retrace their steps or refind a certain object by following the spots they have marked with their own scent glands.

There is a peculiar quality to the spot they make. It holds its scent for a remarkably long time. Long after you have washed off the place where a badger has made its mark, it will still retain the peculiar musty smell that one associates with badgers' sets.

Nikki had two speeds: Very Fast and Stop. Eating and playing fell into the first category. Anything she did not like, such as going for a walk with visitors or meeting strangers, definitely fell into the second. At these times she would appear to be flat out, often lying comatose in her favorite chair by the fire. People who called and wanted to see her often went away with the idea that she was a quiet, passive creature. She might scarcely have moved the whole time they had been there, except for stolidly refusing to vacate her chair.

Those who saw her play, however, could not doubt her real character. She had been playful from the moment her legs had begun to improve, but as the weeks went by, in her play at least, Nikki revealed what she truly was: basically a wild animal. Her play became so boisterous, so intense, that she could no longer be compared to a young puppy.

Tessa had to bear the brunt of her activities. No longer did Nikki try to rouse the setter by playfully pulling the guard hairs on her legs or gently raising and dropping her eyelids. Now she would hurtle into Tessa's sleeping form like a bullet, often tripping herself up by her own exuberance, rolling over and over like a little black and white barrel. Then she would spring onto her feet, prepared to jump at anything that moved. It was as if she were saying, "Now then,

51

who tripped me up in that undignified way?"

If high spirits did not rouse Tessa, Nikki would try the appealing approach. She would bounce round and round the setter, willing her into wakefulness, nickering gently, pleadingly, the whole time.

As a last resort, she would try the cunning approach, creeping up to the dog and snuggling in with her, worming her way into Tessa's curled form. Gently she would snuggle up to her, nose her, give a little bite. Then, with mischief in her every movement, she would give Tessa a short sharp nip that meant business, causing the setter to sit up with a startled yelp. But Nikki was always ready. She would have sprung to her feet the minute she had administered the bite, and there she would be: expectant, alert, poised on those foreshortened legs, ready for any movement that Tessa might make.

Slowly, sleepily, languidly, Tessa would unwind her long limbs. Then, in the same instant, as if telepathically connected like the fox cubs Tessa and I had watched the day Nikki came to us, both animals would begin to run as if their lives depended on it. Occasionally they would run in the same direction, but generally they would run toward each other. Yet their understanding of each other was such that they never collided. It was an extraordinary thing to watch. They would run at such a speed that it seemed impossible for them to avoid a head-on collision, but at the last minute they would veer one way or the other, narrowly missing each other, and continue their ever-tightening circuits. Occasionally Tessa would stretch out her long legs and the badger would shoot like a cannonball straight under her, but generally they passed to one side or the other, and they always seemed to know which side to go on without ever touching, let alone crashing.

The first time they started dashing round and round in this mad way indoors, Mum rushed in to try to stop them. It was useless. They were suddenly in a wild world of their own, and Mum, with her waving and shouting, was just adding to the general melee.

Round and round they would go, Tessa with her great exaggerated bounds, Nikki bouncing up and down in perfect rhythm, all four little feet leaving and landing on the ground at the same time. I estimated that Nikki had to take seven bounces to one of Tessa's bounds, yet there came a time when it was generally Tessa who was the first to tire.

Frequently Nikki would trip over something, her own feet generally, but she never seemed to hurt herself. She would spring up and look accusingly at different things or people in the room, as if they must have been the cause of her downfall, before resuming the frantic chase. When this happened, Tessa would sink to the ground as Nikki stopped, seemingly pleased at the rest. She would pause with her rear end pointing skyward and her chin resting on her forepaws on the ground, stretched out like an elegant "S," her gentle

eyes watchful and alert. Then with one movement the two of them would be off again, round and round and round in their dizzy circles.

This was the usual way the two animals played together, but sometimes they had periods of much rougher play when they would grunt and growl and sound as if they were really injuring each other. It quite frightened Mum, and at first she often tried to separate them. But they were not really hurting each other. Tessa had complete control of the situation, and if Nikki began to get really rough, the dog would cuff her or nip her in such a way that the badger would stop immediately. Obviously the two had developed a deep understanding. They were the best of friends and became quite inseparable.

8

WHENEVER YOU SAW Tessa you would know that Nikki was not far behind. By the end of June, the badger could keep up with the setter, surpassing her, in fact, in staying power. No longer did I have to carry Nikki most of the way home when we went for a walk. I doubt if I could have done so, she had grown so heavy. We reckoned she was about five months old, and in that time she had grown from a tiny thing that could be held in both hands to an animal who could rest her chin on my shoulder with ease when I picked her up. We never actually weighed her—we could never keep her on the bathroom scale long enough—but the hand wavered around the thirty-five pound point. We thought that was about right, although when I did have to carry her she seemed a good deal heavier.

Whenever I was at home, the two animals were near me. Nikki insisted on accompanying me wherever I went. I often tried to get away without her noticing, but I never succeeded. Sometimes she would seem to be fast asleep, and I would creep across the room, but the second I opened the door Nikki would be faithfully at my heel. If she saw that I was doing something not very interesting, she would sometimes return to her favorite easy chair and resume her recumbent position, but generally she would come with me. Thus I had a badger companion when I washed in the mornings, when I dug the vegetable patch for Mum, when I took the milk bottles out, or when I cleaned my shoes each evening.

She loved to sit on my lap; I always had a lapful of badger when I watched television or read a book. Every so often she would peer shortsightedly right up into my face as if she was just making sure I was still there. She loved me to scratch her behind the ears or between the eyes, and when I did this she would stretch out her chin and close her eyes in badger ecstasy.

Her favorite position, though, was stretched right out on my chest, with her little button of a nose pressed hard against my throat. Sometimes she would try to drape herself round the back of my neck, but she never balanced very well there. I do not think my shoulders were broad enough. But this was her favorite position with Mum. Mum used to laugh when Nikki did this and called the badger her fur stole. Dad used to tell her to make the most of it, as it was the nearest she was ever going to get to the real thing.

During the day Nikki attached herself to Mum in exactly the same way that she did to me when I was home from school. She was affectionate to all the family, but at times she was so affectionate to Mum and me that it was almost overwhelming. That was how Nikki was. Everything she did was measured in contrasts: stop or go, fast or slow, like or loathe. There was no rhyme or reason to her behavior. We just learned to accept this as part of her character.

When people called, Nikki usually showed no interest in them at all, but sometimes her reaction was so violent that we had to put her in another room until the visitor had gone. One person who always had an unfortunate effect on her was the vicar. If the vicar was at the door, Nikki would be out of her easy chair and into the hall almost before we had the front door open. She would climb up his legs and pull and tug at his trouser cuffs. Even her after-dinner nap would be disturbed if the vicar called, and if she disappeared during a walk, I could be pretty sure the vicar was on the horizon.

It was funny, the effect he had on Nikki. None of us could imagine the reason for it. He was a well-meaning, elderly fellow who knew very little about animals; in fact, he had no real interest in them. Nikki certainly had an interest in him, though. She was not violent toward him, nor was she friendly. It was difficult to know what she thought of him. She would charge at him as if he were one of her own kind, nipping at his shoes, pulling at his trousers.

She would also try to remove his shoelaces. This was

an embarrassing habit she developed at a very early age. She seemed to have an inborn aversion to shoes with their laces in the proper place, and she could winkle a shoelace out in a matter of seconds with her nimble front paws. She could use those forepaws like little hands, moving each claw independently of its neighbor. Shoelaces were easy meat to her.

We got used to having Dad charging about each morning, letting us know what he thought of the badger in no uncertain terms. Dad always had everything exactly timed so he could leave for work on the dot. At least, he did before we had the badger. Each night he would clean his shoes and leave them ready for the morning. Now each morning he would go to put them on, and there they would be—laceless.

Poor Dad, he never did learn to put his shoes out of Nikki's reach. If it was not his laces that disappeared, it would be the shoes themselves. Anyone hearing Dad on those mornings would never have thought that ours was a happy home. He always called Nikki Mum's badger at such times. The day that he found one of his best shoes actually buried was dreadful. I thought he was going to have a seizure.

Sophie never helped on these occasions. She used to disappear up to her bedroom, and you could hear her giggling behind the closed door, which just made matters worse.

Mum found the easiest thing to do was to keep a stock of spare shoelaces in the kitchen drawer. She had to, for Nikki did not stick to the shoes of the family. Anyone who came to the door presented fair game to the mischievous badger. She developed her shoelace-removing tactics to such a fine art that she would frequently have the laces out and away before the poor victims were through the door. Generally they would laugh politely when they found themselves wallowing in laceless shoes as they tried to take a step forward, and of course there were some people who refused to believe that Nikki had taken them at all. She was so quick and nimble that it was difficult to realize what she'd been up to. I am sure some people thought it was me and not the badger. Mum used to produce spare sets of laces quickly and suggest to our guests that they replace them when they left, but some people were too polite to point out that their laces had gone, and we would not realize they had lost them until we found an extra pair in one of Nikki's favorite hiding places. The milkman was never reluctant to let us know. He would often be shouting out the information before Mum reached the door.

It was particularly unfortunate that this talent of Nikki's developed at just the same time that Dad was trying to release a semitame gray squirrel. Each day the squirrel was getting wilder and it would soon be off, but in the meanwhile it was still centered on our house and it had discovered a fine sport: baiting the milkman.

It would sit on our roof until the milk truck turned

the corner. Then it would whisk down the drainpipe, wait until the milkman's attention was elsewhere, spring onto the milk crates, and start to remove the silver tops from the milk bottles as quick as lightning, continuing until the milkman realized what was happening and gave it a blow with his hat.

For a few weeks that squirrel really tormented our milkman. It would nip along one side of the truck while the milkman was busy at the other and sneak off a top or two before being spotted, or it would wait until the milkman was halfway up the garden path and then jump out of its hiding place and really set to work on the milk tops while his back was turned.

Unfortunately, it had become just too wild to get hold of again, and when Dad tried, it bit him so badly he had to go to the hospital for treatment. It became quite wild in a matter of weeks, however, and eventually returned to the copse where we had tried to release it.

In the meantime our normally quiet-spoken milkman had become a frenzied, gesticulating shouting figure the moment he came near our house. Nikki's shoelace activities were the last straw for him. We had to make arrangements to collect our milk from a cottage nearer the village, for a time at least.

Nikki did not catch Sophie and me out very often. We used to clean our shoes for school in the evenings, and then we would hide them in a cupboard and shut the door firmly. That was fine until Nikki learned to

maneuver the catch with her businesslike forepaws. We came down one day to find that not only were there no laces, there were no shoes. She had discovered her new game: the disappearing shoe.

Sophie and I had to find somewhere that Nikki could not reach. It was not easy. She could climb up anything. There was one safeguard, though. She would nicker so loudly with delight when she reached something she knew she should not have that very often she gave herself away.

Nikki soon developed another game that seemed to give her a tremendous amount of amusement, though her victims somewhat less. This was toe-biting. She greeted a socked foot with such delight that a stranger little suspected what was to follow, and Nikki would be in with a short sharp nip. This never failed to produce a reaction. Nikki would dash round and round in highest delight, nickering the whole time and getting in another crafty bite if the opportunity arose.

My friends provided real sport for her. Mum used to make them take off their wellington boots before they came indoors because she reckoned they'd be muddy, although we used to think they were quite reasonable. Nikki would dash round and round, getting a bite in here and another one there, nickering away excitedly, thrilled to bits with the reaction she was producing. Meanwhile my friends would be high-stepping it round the sitting room as fast as they could go, and we would all have to make a dash for my bedroom and shut the door firmly before Nikki got there herself.

Sophie and I soon had her measure. We always made sure our slippers were ready before we took off our shoes, and the other way round. All the same, Nikki used to get in a nip if we were not quick.

Once again, it was Dad who came off worst. From sheer force of habit he would slip off his dirty shoes or boots at the door and come in and look for his slippers. That was more than an invitation to Nikki, and two or three times a day Dad would be kangaroo-leaping round the kitchen, shouting to all and sundry to come and find his slippers quickly.

Nikki was pretty difficult to catch at these times. Any attempts we made just seemed to excite her all the more. And she was hard to hold if you did catch her. She could wriggle like an eel.

I shall never forget Guy Fawkes Night that year. We had invited a few people back to the house after the village bonfire. Mum and Sophie had been busy all day getting the refreshments ready, and when we got in they went into the kitchen to heat up the soup.

I shall never forget Mum's face when she came back into the sitting room and saw our guests. They were all standing on the chairs, carrying on their conversations as if they always behaved like that in people's houses.

Of course she did not have to look far for the reason. There was Nikki, dashing about beneath the chairs, nickering ecstatically. It had been extremely muddy in the field where the bonfire was, and most of our friends had taken off their boots or shoes when they came into the house. Nikki had never seen such a harvest of toes in her life.

9

MUM WAS MOST ANNOYED when Sophie brought her English book home from school. Sophie had had to write a composition about "Getting ready in the morning." She had written that she had to crawl under Mum's bed so that she could find the soap and washcloth to wash, and that while she was under there she had found the dog's saucepan, Grandad's suspenders, and Mum's new hat that she had bought for a wedding. Sophie continued that she had found the toothpaste behind the cushion on the easy chair in the sitting room, but the tube was a bit chewed up so she did not bother to brush her teeth. She said that she had hidden her shoes under the pillow, but when she got them out the shoelaces had gone, so she had to go and get another pair out of the refrigerator. Mum said that Sophie made ours sound like a terrible house and that people would think we were most peculiar.

The fact is, we often did have to go round the house on this sort of recovery course before we could get ready for anything. And it was quite true about Mum hiding the shoelaces in the fridge. She had been so angry when Nikki managed to open the broom cupboard and find her secret supply that she had hidden the rest of them, herself, in the fridge, remarking that the badger would never think of looking there.

Badgers are well known for their tidy habits, and Nikki was no exception to this rule. In the wild, badgers keep their sets in spotless condition. Anything out of place is removed and discarded. Even a leaf that has blown into the entrance hole or a piece of straw that was dropped when they renewed their bedding will quickly be taken out.

Nikki developed this tidiness characteristic to an extreme. A piece of string, a bit of mud, anything that offended her sense of neatness was quickly gathered and hidden in one of her hiding places. At first Mum thought it was a delightful habit and one that the rest of the family should follow. She soon changed her mind about that, though, because as Nikki increased in size, so did the number of things that she considered out of place. Cushions, antimacassars, even cutlery from the table would be gathered up and hidden in one of her favorite places in an untidy heap. I can remember Mum replacing the antimacassars six or seven times one morning before she gave it up as a bad job.

The picture was much the same upstairs. Mum had to crawl under the bed to recover her make-up, and sometimes her nylons and her underclothes as well, if she had forgotten to close the chest of drawers up tightly.

One day when Aunt Gerty had come to tea, Nikki made a real entrance. She must have found a drawer a little open—Mum was always forgetting to shut them —and she had made the most of the opportunity. She suddenly exploded on us, completely entangled in Mum's underwear. Somehow she had got her head through a bra, and the rest of the garment was trailing along behind her. It kept tripping her up, and each time she tripped she became more and more entangled. Aunt Gerty's face was a study.

Nikki had two favorite hiding places. She stowed most of her acquisitions behind the easy chair in the

living room. Her second favorite place was under Mum's bed. She used to hide herself there as well sometimes, particularly if she had done something naughty like run off with one of Sophie's precious dolls.

That did cause trouble, and Nikki knew that it was wrong. Running off with a doll always caused an uproar. But sometimes the badger seemed to get the devil in her. You could see her little beady eyes twinkling, and with a quick snatch she would be off. She would choose her moments and never stole a doll unless Sophie was around. Sophie would get in a real temper, but there was no shame in Nikki. She would bounce round and round the room, nickering the whole time, as if she were trying to explain to Sophie that it was just a game. Sophie would stamp her feet and start to march out of the room, but invariably Nikki had taken her laces and Sophie would end up sitting on the floor, giggling, with the badger jumping round and round her in great delight, nickering. It sounded as if the two of them were laughing together. They certainly made the same kind of noise.

You can have no idea how tidy our house looked when Nikki lived in it. Dressing tables were cleared regularly, as were all other surfaces that held ornaments or the like. A trail of mauled flowers up the staircase would let us know that Mum's newest flower arrangement was the latest thing to upset Nikki's sense of order. A wail from Sophie would inform us that the badger had had similar feelings about the way she had set the table and had neatly cleared it all off again. Cushions, library books, potted plants, anything that could be moved proved irresistible to that badger. If I put my homework down for a couple of seconds or Dad put his cigarette packet down, they would be whisked away before we had time to realize they were gone.

I shall never forget the day when Nikki attempted to discover whether cigarettes were more than just articles to tidy away. We found her sitting on the stairs, halfway up, an open packet of cigarettes beside her. She had stuck a cigarette into the side of her mouth and was using those capable forepaws to turn it round as if she was trying to find out what Dad found to appreciate in them.

Handbags were another badger delight. Most of our women visitors would deposit their handbags casually on the floor beside them. That really did offend Nikki's tidiness cult, and the bag would be hurried away almost as soon as it was put down. There was generally a great panic when the disappearance was discovered, and Mum would have to make the rounds of Nikki's hiding places in order to restore the bag to the owner.

That was until the affair of Aunt Gerty's bag.

Aunt Gerty believed in outsize handbags. Dad said she used to carry everything in hers except the kitchen sink. She certainly did produce the most peculiar things from it from time to time. One day Mum could not find the can opener, and Aunt Gerty dug into her voluminous handbag and produced one from its depths. Another time she found a cheese sandwich in it when she was looking for something quite different. Dad reckoned the sandwich was so old it was mummified.

Aunt Gerty always plumped herself down in the easy chair that Nikki preferred. On this occasion she started talking as usual while her anatomy was still poised in midair, as it were, and as usual she deposited her bag beside her.

Even I was surprised at the speed of the following sequence of events. Sophie was the first to realize something was amiss. She started to giggle, and we soon saw why. Nikki had come in. I cannot say that she was intelligent enough to know how to put lipstick on properly, but she had certainly had a good try. There were red streaks all over her mask. She knew she had done wrong and tried to worm her way up onto my lap. In the same instant, Aunt Gerty discovered that her bag was missing.

Need I say more? Not only had Nikki taken the bag, her nimble paws had discovered how to undo the catch and she had really gone to town on the contents. Three weeks later we were still recovering Aunt Gerty's belongings from all over the house.

Mum began to think Nikki's neatness was becoming a bit too much of a good thing when she discovered she could not start preparing Sunday lunch until she had crawled under the bed to retrieve the saucepans from the jumble of miscellaneous objects beneath it and found the sausages she had bought for supper there as well. But what finally incensed her was the way Nikki helped her do the gardening.

My mother goes through life in periods of enthusiasms. It was gliding once; another time it was ice skating. Home decorating and dressmaking kept cropping up—not that the latter affected me very much; it was Sophie that had to wear the results. Painting the toilet seat was another recurring passion of Mum's, so it was a bit of a relief when Dad bought a plastic one. At this period, her reigning passion was gardening. At least it was a change from her photography phase.

She had spent the whole day preparing the flower beds, putting in the plants and some special dahlia corms that she had bought. You can well imagine what she thought (and said) when she went up to her room to change and, looking under the bed for her make-up, found everything that she had just planted neatly laid out in three rows. Evidently the plants had offended Nikki's sense of tidiness in some way. She must have been digging them up and carrying them off as quickly as Mum had been planting them.

10

THE WHOLE FAMILY had begun to realize that to keep a badger in the house in the same way that we kept the dogs or cats was fast becoming impracticable. We had a family conference about it one Sunday evening.

Nikki had been boisterous all day. She had sneaked in during lunch time so cunningly that nobody had noticed her. Then suddenly the tablecloth was whipped off with such alacrity that we were all too stunned to save anything that was on it. There sat Mum with the gravy boat literally upside down in her lap, while Dad, at the other end of the table, still had the carving knife and fork raised in the air and a look of incredulity as the roast slid swiftly away from him.

Even Nikki herself was disconcerted at the effect she had caused. She dashed round and round the table, giving little high-pitched squeals, stopping every so often to shake her head. She was spattered from head to toe with gravy and vegetables. Mum was sure she had scalded herself and did not know whether to bemoan the spoiled meal or try to catch Nikki to make sure that she was not hurt. Of course the second impulse prevailed, and we all tried to get hold of the badger, but Nikki was not having any of that. She continued to career round and round the room, finding time to sneak what was left of the Yorkshire pudding and swallow it quickly while she was out of our reach.

In the end Dad pushed her out into the garden. Mum salvaged what she could of the meal and opened a can of fruit for dessert. She put the empty can outside the kitchen door, intending to throw it into the trash can later. We were hardly seated at our resumed meal when there was a resounding crash, followed a few seconds later by another.

I have never known the family to move so quickly. It sounded as if the house was coming down at the very least. There was Nikki dashing around the garden like a thing possessed, with an empty peach can fitted firmly over her head. Obviously the smell of the peaches had been too much for her, and she had gone in search of possible tidbits, getting her head firmly wedged in the can in the process. She was in an absolute panic, dashing round and round, backward and forward. Every time she came to a wall or other impediment she dashed full into it with a crash, for she had completely lost all sense of direction and position. It was not until

she sat down and frantically tried to pull the can off with her nimble forepaws that Dad managed to get hold of her and slide it off. It was a very tight fit.

Nikki still had a lot of growing to do, but we had learned that even a three-quarters-grown badger can disrupt family life in no uncertain way. We knew in our hearts that the best thing for her was to return to the wild. Sophie disagreed, of course. She would have filled her bedroom with all kinds of animals, treating them all like dolls if she could.

We would all have been pleased if Nikki had proved to be a tame, amenable pet, but this was obviously not going to happen. As Nikki was growing, so the characteristics of a truly wild animal were becoming stronger. In any case, was it fair to try to tame an animal that by its very birth had the right to be free? Was it not better to try to return the animal to its rightful surroundings where it could dig at will, burrow, and play with its own kind?

Reluctantly, we decided that Nikki would have to be given freedom. This did not mean just taking her out into the country and dumping her, expecting her to make her own way, as we have known some people to do with wild animals and birds. That can be really cruel: getting an animal used to a steady food supply and a stable warm home and then just deserting it in a strange spot, completely out of reach of everything it has learned to accept.

No, in order to prepare Nikki for freedom, we would allow her to develop the wilder side of her character. We would let her root round more when we took her for walks through the woods, encourage her to dig, to search out roots and insects, take her down to the places where we knew the wild badgers could be found. The first thing, however, was to fit up a run outside for her, so that later we could let her out at night and she could return if and when she was hungry.

Dad and I designed a run that we thought would satisfy both Mum's sense of what would look decent and Nikki's natural instincts. We intended to make it twelve feet by six by five, with a barrel-like structure at one end which was the nearest we could get to a real set. We would never have kept an animal permanently in a run of this size, but for a sleeping area, or a place to banish Nikki to when she had tried our patience just a little too much, these dimensions seemed adequate. A place to confine Nikki would be most important soon. Tessa was pregnant and dogs do not usually tolerate other animals around their pups. Dad promised to order the wood and wire the next day so that the two of us could start on it at the weekend.

The whole scheme was precipitated when it suddenly dawned on Mum that Tessa's pups were a little more imminent than she had calculated. The setter had snapped at Nikki a couple of times during the day, and each time we had shut the badger in the other room, thinking she was getting too boisterous. Now the setter made a beeline for the badger and really savaged her. Nikki had been lying on the hearthrug, sleeping. She made no attempt to retaliate and slunk backward, completely cowed by Tessa's onslaught.

"I think we'd better get somewhere fixed up for Nikki right away rather than leave it until next weekend," Dad said.

For want of anything better, we had to banish Nikki to the outside toilet. How she objected! She scratched the door and screamed in fury. I had made it comfortable for her and put in a large box with plenty of clean straw and a large cloth. She quieted down a bit when I put food and water in for her, but only for a short while. Throughout the night there were spasmodic outbursts of temper vented on that toilet door. I am sure the neighbors wondered what was going on.

We had already prepared the shed at the top of the garden for Tessa, and we carried her box up there. She settled in it immediately and gave me a great appreciative lick all down the side of my face.

We did not need to go outside the next morning to know that Mum's calculating had been way off. We could hear the faint whimpering as soon as we opened the back door. Tessa's puppies had been born during the night; six gray and pink, helpless, wriggling, blind little things. Tessa was enormously pleased with herself. She licked the small creatures protectively and stared up at us proudly.

Nikki was frantic by this time. She knew something was going on, and she had not been included. She was not prepared to put up with the indignity. She banged against the door until the whole frame shook. When I did open it, the badger shot out like a cork from a champagne bottle and ended up right across the garden, sitting on her bottom and looking very surprised.

She was very suspicious. She was determined that she was not going to be left out again. She stuck to me like a limpet, studying everything with the greatest care.

Tessa's disappearance mystified her. She sniffed repeatedly round the setter's favorite spots. She carried the very deflated ball out into the garden (we had thought the ball was lost, but Nikki must have known where it was all the time) and nickered invitingly, but no dog came out to join her.

Tessa was far too concerned with her maternal duties for the first two or three days to spare a thought for the badger, but one morning she forced herself away and came out into the garden, stretching her long limbs languidly. Nikki charged her. She was so pleased to see her that I think even Tessa was taken aback by the force of the welcome. The setter was too much of a matriarch now, however, to respond in kind, and she surveyed the enthusiastic young badger in a most condescending way.

Nikki continued to bounce round and round her, nickering in complete delight, and finally Tessa bowed down low on her forepaws. For a second or two the animals touched noses, then they were off, round and round the garden, tripping over here, rolling over there, dashing round in their accustomed fashion. Then Tessa, suddenly tired, sank down on her haunches. No amount of badger cajoling could coax her into move-ment again. It was as if her attention was suddenly on a different wave length. She turned her back on the badger and returned to her pups, whose hungry cries of welcome were quite strong already. Nikki sat down and surveyed the shed, looking every inch like a picture of love locked out.

We had fitted a special gate to the shed. Tessa with her long legs could climb over it with ease, but it kept the badger out. Nikki soon realized where Tessa was when she disappeared so regularly. She would stand at that gate with her nose pressed firmly against the wire, nickering imploringly.

11

ONE MORNING I went out to call Nikki before I went to school. She had been playing happily with my old football, worrying it and shaking it like a pup playing with a slipper. Generally I put her back in her den when I went to change into my school uniform. Her run was proving more difficult to build than Dad and I had envisaged, so she was still occupying the outside toilet. She was always a bit dubious about going back in, but I used to put her food in there. Once that ever-twitching nose caught a whiff of the breakfast leftovers, she was in like a rotund rocket, and it was a race to close the door before she had cleared the plate.

On this particular day, she had been playing so contentedly that I had left her while I ran in to change. When I came back, the garden was empty. The football lay, deflated and misshapen, in the middle of the lawn, but there was no sign of Nikki. There was no response to my calling. I suppose I must have panicked, because I ran up and down the hedgerow, looking in every spot that could have concealed a half-grown badger. I ran indoors and searched every likely and unlikely hiding place. Nikki had vanished.

I could not go off to school not knowing what had become of her. Mum and Sophie came out to have a look round. I could see that they were worried as well.

Then Sophie called, "She was here all the time!"

There she was, snuggled in with Tessa and the pups. She must have clambered up the wire and over the top of the gate, for it was still in place. I nearly cried with relief.

Then it was Sophie that panicked.

"Nikki will bite those pups if you don't get her out," she shouted, "and she could kill them, you know."

I stepped over the wire into Tessa's domain and picked up the errant badger by the scruff of her neck. Of course, Sophie objected to my picking her up like that, although it is the way that badgers pick up their young. Nikki objected too. She growled, a low rumbling growl that grew from the base of her throat. It was a noise that sounded menacing, although it was no louder than the noises she made at Tessa when they played together. But this was no playful growl; it meant business. Then, without further warning, she turned her head and snapped at me. For a second she was not the animal we knew, but a wild, hostile creature. Her small beady eyes looked evil, and her lips were drawn back from those strong white teeth, showing that they could do damage.

Fortunately she was unable to gain much purchase, for I had her firmly by the scruff. All the same, she had given me a nasty bite on the lower part of my arm,

drawing blood and giving me a bruise that took weeks to heal and turned every color of the rainbow before it did.

If you keep pets, they have to learn to live in the surroundings that you provide. Certainly we could not allow Nikki to use her teeth in this way without chastisement, for what would she bite the next time? A hit was something she would understand, something her own parents would have administered. So I hit her. Sophie did not like that either. I gave the badger one short sharp rap across the nose, where she was sensitive. It hurt her and made her eyes water. She brushed her nose with her forepaw and shook her head. I showed her my arm so that she would associate the bite with the punishment and see the damage she had done. She understood. She tucked her head down into her body and made no attempt to bite me again.

Then I ran to look at the pups. They were fine.

When I got home from school that day, I let Nikki out before I changed. I did wonder if she would hold that hit against me and be more difficult to handle. If anything, the reverse was true. She came trotting out, muttering away, and squatted on my feet with a real possessiveness which she had not shown before. Then she climbed up my leg and I picked her up. She rested her chin on my neck and sighed a great deep sigh. I am sure it was her way of saying she was sorry.

She came in while I changed, then went out with me into the garden and played on the grass with that peculiarly shaped football. Suddenly, she stopped playing and cocked her head to one side as if she were thinking. She had remembered Tessa and the pups. She tackled that wire door as other adventurers have tackled Mount Everest. Scrambling up one side, she stood precariously at the top. Then, losing her balance, she tumbled ignominiously to the ground.

She hurried busily over to the recumbent family and pushed her way right into the center of the group. I watched her carefully. I was not sure what to do or how she would behave. I expected her to show some kind of jealousy toward the pups or treat them as intruders, but her behavior was impeccable. I was never really happy when the badger was in with the dogs, at least while the puppies were so small, but no harm came to them.

As they grew up, a peculiar relationship developed between them and the half-grown badger. Nikki became a kind of self-appointed, honorary nursemaid. She never attempted to harm the pups in any way, although she was very firm with them at times, particularly when they were too boisterous. She did not annoy Tessa either.

It seemed no time at all before the pups were beginning to venture out into the garden. They were very cautious at first, and any unusual noise or movement would send them scurrying back to their familiar shed. Nikki would try to encourage them by bouncing round in her usual rowdy fashion. When her behavior caused the complete opposite of what she had in mind, she would plump herself down in the middle of the garden and appear completely nonplussed.

One day all the pups were sitting on the path watching their mother and Nikki dash round in one of their usual Grand Prix circuits. Suddenly the largest dog pup joined in, and then another and another until only one little quiet bitch puppy remained sitting. Of course, the pups did not have the stamina to keep up. They kept dropping out in turn to regain their breath before resuming the mad dash again for a few more seconds. In no time at all, the youngsters had worn themselves out and just lay exhausted where they had stopped, leaving us with a setter-covered lawn.

But that was just the start. There was no stopping the pups now. They were always ready to join in the games, although these were of short duration. Nikki was delighted. If she could not coax Tessa into movement, she could always rely on some response from at least one of the pups.

It did not take them long to seek out the badger when they were feeling lively. Under Nikki's guidance, the pups soon learned to dig up the few dahlia corms Mum had saved from Nikki's attentions in the first place. Nikki found that those pups could demolish slippers and shoes in no time. Nor did it stop there. The badger, realizing what good sport these miscellaneous objects provided for the pups, took to depositing all her spoils out on the lawn rather than stowing them away in one of her hiding places. Those pups were quite extraordinarily destructive. A tube of toothpaste would be devoured in a second or two, hairbrushes and washcloths chewed up in a matter of minutes. It took a little longer to shred a towel or bedspread, but now that Nikki had found a real objective for her collecting mania, her ambitions knew no bounds. One day Mum caught Nikki dragging the eiderdown quilt from her bed downstairs. The badger did not, however, get the chance to discover what sport that would have provided for the pups!

Nikki herself was not destructive with the household things. No doubt she could have been, but she seemed to have the intelligence to know what she could and could not do. She just provided the means. The pups needed no encouragement to do the rest. Nikki would sit innocently on the side, watching them out of those little beady mischievous eyes.

Then she found a new delight. She could get out of the garden through some holes at the bottom of the hedge. So could the pups. The day Nikki discovered this, she led all six pups out into the paddock at the end of the garden, pursuing all kinds of enticing smells. Poor Tessa tried to force her great length through one hole in the hedge after another. She barked commandingly, but the pups ignored their mother and ambled happily after Nikki. Nikki sniffed and dug, turning over this stone or that loose turf. The six little pups followed obediently until they became either too tired or bored, and then they dropped out one at a time.

Tessa sat down at the end of the garden and wailed. It was the most mournful sound I have ever heard.

We were hunting pups the whole afternoon.

The weak little bitch had gone only a few feet from the end of the garden before giving up. She was quickly reunited with her mother. Tessa licked her violently. After much searching, three more were found in clumps of high grass. Eventually we found another over near the farm dairy. Of the sixth there was not a sign. We looked everywhere. Nikki, of course, had long since returned to the garden and was sitting on the path washing herself, completely unconcerned about the worry she had caused. Tessa refused to help. She was busy licking her pups time and time again, despite their protests at her thorough treatment. She was so delighted to have those five back that she did not realize that there was still one to come.

Just when we were beginning to despair of ever finding the truant, one of the farm workers came up the hill with the pup in his arms. He had found it wandering down in the village. We were lucky it had not been run over; there is quite a lot of traffic through our one road on weekends.

We reinforced the hedge immediately, but this did not thwart Nikki. She soon dug beneath it, and a hole that was big enough for a badger was big enough for a pup. Several times we had to organize puppy searches because the pups had followed Nikki out on one of her adventures, leaving their mother wailing hopelessly in the garden. However, we now knew what the matter was as soon as the setter started up, and we did not give the pups a chance to get so far again.

When the pups were about six weeks old, Nikki learned how to open the refrigerator. The first time Mum came downstairs and found the puppies finishing off the roast while Nikki watched them with a proprietary air, she thought that she must have left the door ajar. The next day they made a real mess with two pounds of butter. The day after that we found Nikki sitting at the side of the lawn with the six pups each chewing happily on a rasher of bacon. The badger had not kept any for herself but had distributed her spoils with generosity and sat watching the busily chewing pups with real pride.

Mum refused to believe that Nikki was opening the fridge. It had a heavy door and Mum herself found it quite stiff to open. Then she caught Nikki at it. The badger came busily into the kitchen, looked warily around the room, then hurried across to the fridge. There, she lay down on the floor on her back and carefully inserted her two nimble forepaws into the narrow crack between the door and the fridge itself. Mum could see her tensing her muscles as she pulled. The door sprang open and Nikki was into the fridge, all of her, in a trice.

Dad tried wedging a heavy object against the door,

but this did not stop Nikki. She had surprising strength for her size and could lever it open with ease. In the end, Dad had to contact the factory and ask them to make a shield for the fridge to stop a badger opening it. They were intrigued with his request; they had never been asked for anything like that before. They quickly produced a shield which did the trick, a long strip of silver metal which fitted the length of the fridge. We still have it. After all, you never know.

12

WE SAW the departure of the puppies with very mixed feelings. Sophie cried, of course, every time that somebody came and took one away. They were seven weeks old when the first one was sold. This was the weak little bitch, and we were pleased to see her go to a good home. All the others went abroad, except for the one we kept ourselves, so we kept the five others until they were at least ten weeks old and strong enough to face fairly long air journeys.

Gradually the parade I took for a walk each evening became shorter. At first all eight animals came out with me. They kept strictly in line, each one in its allotted place: first Nikki, walking so closely to heel that I had to tread very carefully, then Tessa with her great loping steps, followed by her pups. The timid little bitch always brought up the rear. But it seemed no time at all before we were left with just Nikki, Tessa, and the one pup we had decided to keep.

Tessa was quite her old self again. From the way she behaved, you would not have thought she had ever had

90

any pups. She did not seem much more than a pup herself at times. She certainly could not have cared less about the puppy we were keeping. But Nikki cared. It seemed that she had given herself the job of showing it what was what. The badger rooted busily round the garden with the inquisitive little puppy trotting along behind her. They would wander off into the paddock together, but we had no need to worry now, because they could both find their way home without any trouble.

It seemed quite understandable that Silver, as we called the pup, should begin to pick up many of the badger's habits. She would dig at the same mouseholes, turn over the same stones that captured Nikki's attention. She even ran off a couple of times with items she had stolen and hid them behind the easy chair, in just the same way that the badger did. But we did not realize how much influence Nikki was having on that puppy, though I do not know what we could have done if we had. I am sure now that Nikki's influence caused Silver to develop as she did.

Silver was nearly four months old when she ran off the first time. We eventually found her up at the farm. After that, we never knew who would phone up telling us that they had found our puppy or where the call would come from.

Once again we strengthened the fencing round the garden, but we could not keep Silver in. She became adept at digging, and if she could not get beneath the fence quickly, the badger was always close by to lend a paw. Silver also developed a stealthy cunning she must surely have learned from Nikki. She would be sitting in the garden, looking the picture of obedience. Turn your back for a second and she would be away, so swiftly, so silently that it would be several minutes at least before you noticed she was gone.

The time came when she could not accept restriction of any kind. Perhaps we were at fault in allowing her too much freedom when she was young. We tied her on a running line, but she nearly went mad. She worked herself up to such a frenzy she began to foam at the mouth, and I got frightened and let her loose. We could never take Silver out in the car as we did Tessa and Nikki. She would be intrigued with the journey for the first couple of miles. She would sit up on the back seat with her chin down on her chest, looking down her nose at everything around her, the very picture of her mother. But then she would go crazy, frantic to get out. Shutting her in a shed had the same effect, and she would scratch at the door until her paws bled. Normally she was a good-natured little pup, but if she was restricted or shut up in any way, she immediately became a frantic, crazed beast. We tried firmness, kindness, rewarding her with food; we even hit her, but we could not break her of roaming.

One day the squire stopped Dad. He said that he did not really mind having guests at breakfast, but he had had our pup sitting beside him at breakfast every morning for the last ten days, looking up at him with large soulful eyes, following every morsel that he put into his mouth with a deep sigh. It had reached the point where he was beginning to feel guilty about eating his own meal.

The farmer stopped Mum the same day. He was very nice about it. He said he had no doubt that Silver thought she was helping, but whenever he brought the cows in for milking, the pup was always there, walking behind him, nosing at the heels of every lagging animal. She helped when the cows were taken back to the field afterward as well. The only trouble was that she seemed to be under the impression that he was not milking them often enough. She kept rounding them up and bringing them in at all times of the day. The previous day, Silver had escorted the herd proudly into the yard no less than six times. If she could not get them through the gate, she just rounded them up into a corner of the field and sat down and barked and barked until somebody came to admire her work. The farmer said he wasn't exactly worried—Silver never did any harm—but it was beginning to affect the milk yield, and he would appreciate it if we would do something about it.

That same evening Sophie found Silver at the village shop, sitting beside the children as they came out with candy or ice cream, looking up at them appealingly, giving such hungry whines that each of them in turn gave her some tidbit or other. Sophie was furious when

she saw the pup. Silver knew she was doing wrong. She sank onto the ground with her head resting on her forepaws, looking up at Sophie as if to say, "Don't be angry with me, please." But the lady in the shop said that the pup was down there every evening about the same time when the children were around with their pennies. "She hasn't missed a day for a fortnight," she said.

Dad and I took Silver along to the gamekeeper's that evening and persuaded him to try to train the pup for us. We did not want her trained as a highly efficient gun dog. We just wanted a dog that would be obedient, a dog we could live with.

In the following weeks we called over once or twice. The keeper was delighted with her. She was responding well to training and was one of the best bitches he had ever had, he reckoned.

We went over to see her one Sunday morning. She was fine and sat there looking at us, her noble head cocked a little to one side in just the same way that Tessa held her head.

That evening the keeper phoned. Silver was dead.

It turned out that he had taken her for the next step in her training. She had to sit when told and stay there while the keeper walked away. She was not to follow or go to him until he called. Silver waited there, alert, intelligent. Then, when the trainer was a good hundred yards from her and actually turning round, she ran. He said it was as if she had been obedient and responsive all the time but really only waiting for the opportunity to go free.

When a dog disobeys in this way, the trainer tries to stay with the dog and be there when it gives up. Then the dog must be punished, either while it is actually doing wrong or the moment it has given up, so that it can associate the punishment with the wrongdoing.

"One short, sharp tap across the nose is often enough," the keeper told us. "It is no good letting any time lapse, because the animal will have forgotten what it has done or not understand why it is being punished. It must associate the punishment with the crime. I flatter myself," he added, "that I can keep up with most dogs, but I couldn't even keep that young bitch of yours in sight. It ran like a thing possessed."

She must have run and run, because she suddenly broke through the hedge onto the main road into Winchester, about three miles away from the keeper's house. A car coming along hit her straight on, and she was killed immediately. Judging from the time she left the keeper and the time at which she was killed, we think that she must have kept on running in a dead straight line without a stop.

Looking back now, I do not think we would ever have cured Silver of this tendency to run off. I think it was too much part of the animal herself. How much was inbred, however, and how much was Nikki's influence we shall never know, but I have often wondered.

13

NIKKI, TOO, had a marked tendency to run off.

The first time it happened I did not realize she had gone. I had become so used to her walking really close to my heel that I rarely bothered to turn round and check that she was still there. On this day the three of us had gone out for a walk, Nikki and Tessa and I. It suddenly dawned on me that I was not feeling the usual gluelike pressure on my heel. I turned round to find that Nikki had disappeared.

I could not think what might have happened to her. I searched and I called. I even stopped a couple of complete strangers who were obviously out for a day's hike and asked them if they had seen a lost-looking badger running back along the road. I think they thought I was a bit peculiar. They gave a very guarded reply before they hurried on.

In the end I just sat on a stump of a tree near the spot where I had last seen her and waited, hoping that any minute I would hear the undergrowth rustling and see her busy little form come into view. But there was nothing, just silence, the absolute, utter silence that one can only know and understand when one lives in the country.

I must have sat there for over an hour. In the end I went home, depressed and despondent, quite convinced that something dreadful had happened to the badger. There was no other reason for her to disappear so completely.

Imagine how I felt when I went into the sitting room and found the corner easy chair half-full of a reclining badger, leaning back nonchalantly and absent-mindedly scratching her stomach with her paw.

"We wondered where you were," Sophie said brightly. "Nikki's been home for ages."

No one seemed a bit worried about me or the state I was in. Dad, in fact, was delighted with the whole thing.

"Can't you see," he said, "that we need not worry any more? Now that she's found her own way home once, she can do it again."

Nikki disappeared several times after that, but I never worried about her until I checked to see if she had gone home by herself. Leastways, I *say* I never worried, but there was always a horrible uneasy feeling in the pit of my stomach until I actually saw her alive and well again. Sometimes I would set off for home, feeling really cross that she had disappeared again and had not come when I called her, only to find that she had materialized and was walking to heel without my realizing she was there.

I became so used to finding her ensconced in her favorite chair, after she had disappeared without a trace, that the day I got home and she was not there gave me a terrific shock. I dashed back the way I had come, through the gate and down the slope, and met her at the corner. She was bouncing along, all four feet off the ground at the same time, moving with such perfect rhythm that you could have fitted any rousing march to her movement. She did not seem to have a care in the world. Certainly she did not falter when she saw me but carried on up the short hill at the same steady gait. Up the hill and through the gate she went. I do not know why I bothered to worry.

One day, however, she did not come home. We had been walking up through the copse where the silver fox has its den. Years ago there was a silver fox farm in the village, and Dad thinks that the fox living up in the copse now must be a descendant of one that escaped twenty years or so ago.

Nikki had disappeared before we reached the fallen oak, but I was not worried about her. As Tessa and I started down toward the track, my attention was suddenly caught by a dark movement in the sky. Then there was another; two dark birds flashed downward before they spread their wings and were borne skyward like wind-blown swansdown, only lifting their primary feathers from time to time to send them up. These were hobbies. Dad had seen them and had said that he thought they must be nesting near the village. Now I watched completely spellbound as they dived and soared, spun and hovered, plucking moths and insects from the air as they flew, discarding unwanted wings and body cases to flutter uselessly toward the ground while they devoured the tidbits in flight. It was a fantastic sight. Of all birds, hobbies must be the most beautiful on the wing, and I watched an aerial ballet which was pure poetry in motion for a good half hour or more.

At last Tessa and I wandered homeward, expecting to find Nikki in her usual chair. But we didn't get there.

I knew that Nikki hadn't gone home as soon as we reached the end of the village and heard the noise coming from Waverly Cottage. I sensed it was Nikki and ran toward that cottage faster than I have ever moved in my life. The front door was open, and I did not stop to knock, especially as the noise was reaching a fantastic volume. Sure enough, I could hear Nikki's excited nickering joining in the general hullabaloo, so I dashed right through into the living room.

The first thing I saw was two portly women balanced precariously about three feet above floor level, shouting fit to bust. Miss Langtree was poised on the back of the sofa, which was swaying backward and forward as her weight caused it to tip. Her friend was balanced on the windowsill, hanging onto the curtains for extra support. If anything, she was a bit heavier than Miss Langtree. Both were screaming at the tops of their voices. I have never heard a noise like it. It was terrific.

So was the mess. A low table in front of the fire still had a few remnants of a meal on it. The rest was scattered mainly on the hearthrug, although some bits seemed to have taken off at a somewhat greater range. In fact, it was difficult to walk across the room without picking up the odd piece of bread and butter on one's shoes. Ham sandwiches and chocolate cake do not look at all appetizing when they have been spread across the floor and trodden on for good measure, but Tessa did not let that hamper her. Regardless of the furore going on around her, she waded into those sandwiches, or what was left of them, with enthusiasm.

The cause of the disturbance with obvious. A very, very exuberant badger was jumping up at her reluctant hostess, offering her the remains of a very, very dead rat. I smelled it before I saw it. Obviously Miss Langtree had, too, and her reaction had not been the one the generous badger was expecting. Nikki was running between the two women, thrusting the rat at each of them in turn. The more the two women screamed, the more eager the badger became to deposit her offering before them. She was trying to scramble up the wall to reach Miss Langtree. I called her frantically, but my voice only seemed to make her more excited, and she dashed between the two of them faster and faster.

Then, as I watched, Nikki scrambled up the back of the sofa with her smelly offering and began to dash along it. Miss Langtree's screaming had reached a crescendo when suddenly the whole lot collapsed, depositing the lady flat on her back on the hearthrug, chocolate cake and all. Nikki, making the most of the situation, hurried forward and deposited the odious rat in the region of Miss Langtree's stomach, then disappeared casually out of the front door as if her mission had been accomplished.

I tried to apologize to the two women, but they did not seem to appreciate it, so I beat a hasty retreat. Tessa refused to follow immediately. She had no intention of letting all that lovely food go to waste, and I had to pull her off the remains of the sandwiches.

When I got home I just collapsed in a chair. I could not stop laughing. Mum had to shake me to find out what it was all about. She did not think it was at all funny when I told her. In fact, she was so concerned she got out her coat and ran down the hill to the cottage to see if she could help.

She made me go down the next day to say that I was sorry, although it was not really my fault. I took Nikki with me. She walked closely to heel and was ever so obedient. I wanted Miss Langtree and her friend to see that she was not always so boisterous. Miss Langtree did not seem very pleased to see me or the badger. In fact, she did not invite either of us into the house, though she is not a bit like that ordinarily. She is one of those hospitable people who usually have the cookie jar handy. I gathered that she did not mind if she never saw Nikki again, and, what was more, her friend had no wish to see either the badger or me.

It was just after this that Mr. Cass called.

Mr. Cass was one of the village characters, a retired police inspector who certainly knew what was what. He lived about a mile from the village in a delightful spot with views looking right down the Meon Valley. He was a great gardener, and his garden was always a riot of color, a haven of peace.

Nikki soon changed that.

It appeared Mr. Cass had a wasps' nest in the garden. Would I take the badger up there to clear it out? He had read that badgers dug out wasps' and bees' nests, and he could show us along the bank by the wood where one had been dug out by wild badgers a short while before. (In fact, we did go up later on and saw how neatly the wild badgers had dug away the earth around—to reveal the perfectly shaped delicate cone of the wasps' nest.)

This wasps' nest in Mr. Cass's garden was somewhere around his flower beds. He was sure Nikki would find it. It was a lovely summer's day, so we went up there that afternoon, Nikki and Tessa and I.

Mr. Cass met us and pointed out roughly where he thought we would find the wasps. There were certainly enough of them buzzing around, and they seemed to increase in density near the fence. I took Nikki over in that general direction, but she seemed far more interested in all the exciting new smells than in the small black and yellow insects. Then, purely by chance, she found the hole at the edge of the lawn. Nikki stuck her nose firmly down it and blew.

"Gosh," I thought, "this is going to work!"

Nikki dug a little and stuck her nose down again. Then she retreated a few steps backward. She brushed her nose quickly with her nimble forepaw. Then, without warning, she turned tail and fled. One or two wasps had come out, but Nikki was not waiting to see any more.

Tessa thought she was missing something and ambled over to the hole. She cocked her head on one side as setters do and studied it. Then she, too, thrust her nose down it.

Within seconds she was covered, her entire length one mass of small angry wasps. I tried frantically to brush them out of her long hair and at the same time keep an eye on the swarm, which was steadily increasing in size. In a moment Tessa must have been stung, for she sprang upward with a startled yelp. I had never seen her move so fast. She took to her heels and was off down the lane after Nikki before I had time to gather my wits together.

I could see Mr. Cass peering out at me, his nose pressed firmly against a firmly shut window, and had time to notice that he had made sure all the other windows were shut as well. The buzzing of the wasps was growing noisier and noisier. It is difficult to estimate the numbers of anything that doesn't stay still, but there were an awful lot of those wasps, and the swarm seemed to be growing bigger every second. I did not wait to see how big it would become. Deciding that discretion was the better part of valor, I ran. I followed Nikki and Tessa down the lane, and I do not think I slowed down until I had turned in at our own front gate and was indoors with the door shut firmly behind me.

Dad was working in the garden, putting up a temporary run for a nestful of half-grown gray squirrels that had been brought in that day. He said later that he had wondered whatever was happening. First the garden gate was thrown open, and the badger tore up the garden path and through the back door as if her very life depended on it. A few seconds later the gate was flung back again, and Tessa repeated the exercise. Some five minutes later the gate was flung open again, and there I was, puffing up the path.

I threw myself down on my bed to regain my breath. Nikki was cowering beneath it, and what was more, she was staying there. She refused to budge until teatime, when the smell of food drove all other thoughts from her mind. As for Tessa, Mum and I were pulling wasps from her coat for a good two hours, and she had many nasty stings, particularly round the head.

I never did learn if Mr. Cass got rid of that wasps' nest or not, but I know he has not forgotten that afternoon. He never bothers to say hello when he sees me now; he just asks if I feel like going wasp hunting, then laughs with a great, deep, evil-sounding bellow.

We used to take Tessa and Nikki everywhere with us. Tessa had always loved to go out in the car, and Nikki soon learned to appreciate it, too. The only trouble with Nikki was that she liked to go fast. If we had to slow down for traffic lights or to turn a corner, she would sit up on the back seat and nicker away in annoyance.

We became used to having her along, and we often forgot that there was anything unusual in having a badger walking to heel in a London street or wherever we happened to be. A man stopped me once and told me I ought to keep my dog on a lead in a town. He meant Nikki. There was no need. In any strange place, she stuck to us like wallpaper.

One day Mum went down to the station to meet Grandma, who was coming to stay. Without thinking, Mum called Tessa and Nikki, and the three of them went down to town.

Grandma did not seem too happy about sharing a car with a badger, but she was too polite to say anything. Nikki seemed to sense that she was not appreciated and suddenly appeared on Mum's lap. This would have been all right, had she sat still, but she kept trying to push her little black nose against Mum's. Mum had to shove her off. Nikki then went and sat on Mum's feet. Mum appreciated that even less and pushed her off again, whereupon Nikki proceeded to sit *under* her feet. The trouble was that this meant she was sitting under the pedals as well, and Mum had just started to come down Trinity Hill.

The farm foreman who was standing on the first corner said he had never seen anything like it, and that it was lucky there did not happen to be any other traffic on the road just then. The car kangarooed down the hill. Mum had managed to get the brake pedal halfway down before the uncooperative badger pushed it up again. Then the steering wavered dangerously from side to side as Mum bent down and tried to drag the resisting badger out. Just as they got to the sharp corner at the foot of the hill, Nikki came out of her own accord, and the situation was saved.

I do not know what Grandma thought about the adventure. She never did *say* anything, but I noticed that she always asked if Dad would meet her after that.

14

THERE WAS no denying now that Nikki was no longer a sweet little black and white animal, an amusing, attractive family pet. She was a wild animal in captivity, with the nature and instincts of a wild animal daily becoming stronger.

From the beginning we had tried to encourage her to be good-tempered and to persuade her to accept interruptions during meals. Now, to disturb her while she was eating was to court disaster, for she would turn and bite, and she meant business. She knew it was wrong to bite in this way. Afterward she would always run and squat on our feet and rub her nose against our legs as if she were trying to apologize, but Nikki's bites were now no joke.

Occasionally when she and Tessa were playing together she would bite the setter a little too ferociously, making her yap, especially if Tessa were getting the better of the game, as she often did because she could use her height to such an advantage. Nikki always fussed round Tessa, too, if she hurt her, but there was no hiding the fact that when things did not completely suit her the badger's first reaction was to use those strong, powerful teeth.

We warned people when they called that we did not thing it advisable for them to try to fondle Nikki. That is all we could do—advise. People would see us handling animals and birds and think that they could come in and do exactly the same. They did not appreciate that it takes months and sometimes years of trust and understanding to build up a certain relationship between animal and owner. The animal will not and cannot simply transfer that trust to another human being. This is true of all animals. It is unusual for a dog to behave in the same way toward other people as it does toward those that have reared it. This trait is quite pronounced in domesticated animals and much more pronounced in wild animals, as Nikki showed us.

An acquaintance called in one day with a group of about twenty young people. They were not really interested in animals, and we were not pleased to see them. We had not expected them, and they had called at a most inconvenient time. Mum said, "For goodness' sake, go and talk to them until I can get out."

Nikki was playing in the garden, digging up the filthiest old bone you can imagine. Each evening she dug it up, and each morning Tessa buried it with a great show of indignation. It had become quite a ritual and an accepted game between them. When she saw the strangers, the badger ran and squatted on my feet.

Then, sensing that she was the center of interest, she began to show off. She dashed round and round the garden in such contagious excitement that Tessa joined her. Then she butted one of the youths, bouncing backward immediately as if she were inviting him to join in. The lad rubbed his shins, and I was not surprised, for Nikki could hurt when she butted. Like all her kind, she had an exceptionally hard head. Then she ran toward me, and, rolling onto her back, she started dabbing at me with her forepaws.

"I wouldn't touch her," I warned our friend.

"Oh, I'm used to badgers," he said airily, and, bending over, he rubbed Nikki roughly up and down on her tummy.

The badger bit. She held onto his arm with her two forepaws, and she bit, and she meant it.

The visitor had on a heavy sports coat, but Nikki bit right through it. I could not prise her teeth apart. Luckily, Mum heard me shouting and came out to give me a hand. We had to hold Nikki's nose tightly before she would loosen her hold, and even then it was as much as the two of us could do to get the animal off. She would have been back at him again if she had been given half a chance. We heard afterward that the young man had had to have several stitches in his arm.

Young children were difficult visitors, too. They would always try to stroke Nikki, and often their mothers would encourage them to do so. This horrified Mum. She cannot understand mothers who let their children go up to or touch strange animals without first finding out if it is safe. I thought Nikki would have been all right with really small children. She seemed to understand that they were young and was wonderfully long-suffering when anyone called with toddlers or babies. But after she had turned on this young man and bitten him so badly, we never dared risk it. When strangers called, particularly if they had children, we would get Nikki back into her run.

We had finished the run at last, much to everyone's relief because it meant we could start using the outside toilet again. In a way we were sorry, though, because Nikki had developed the remarkable habit of using that toilet herself, quite properly. Originally I had put a litter box out for her, and I was a bit disturbed to find that she was not using it. I thought there must be something wrong with her. Imagine my astonishment on opening the door one day to find Nikki sitting on the toilet and using it. Of course, Mum was worried when I told her. She thought that the badger might fall into the bowl and not be able to get out. Dad fixed a bit of wire across the top and under the seat to prevent any accident, but considering Nikki's agility, I think Mum was unduly nervous.

When we transferred Nikki to her proper run, I gave her two dishes of water, one of which she always used as a toilet. If she was out in the garden and wanted to make a mess she always ran across and used a drain. She would never make a mess just anywhere. Badgers

in the wild are quite as clean as this. They will never soil in their sets; they dig a series of holes which they use as toilets. When one is full they dig out another and use that.

Nikki's exuberance was phenomenal. She always had been inquisitive and lively. Multiply that by ten, and you have some idea of her energy as she grew older. She was never tired, always ready for a walk, always prepared to investigate another hole or interesting stone. Dad said that she was going through a puppy stage, as all animals do, and once through it she would be a much quieter animal.

Not everyone appreciated the badger's superabundant high spirits, and Mum had one or two letters from people saying that she had no right to keep a wild animal as a pet. One letter really upset her. It was anonymous, of course; that sort always are. It said that Mum was a wicked woman, bringing up children with a badger in the house. It went on and on in that strain. Dad said that Mum was stupid to let letters like that worry her, and that people who wrote them must be mental cases anyway, but they did upset her. She said they got right under her skin and made her wonder if she had done the right thing in keeping Nikki alive in the first place.

We knew she had done the right thing. You could not doubt that when you looked at the badger. If anything, she looked healthier than the wild badgers we liked to watch at dusk. Her coat was glossy and clean, her eyes bright and alert; her every movement suggested good health and high spirits.

I often took her down to the woods and tried to get her to look down the badger holes. I hoped that she would get used to the smell and begin to develop a desire to return to the wild. She was never happy there, though, and always seemed relieved when we turned to go home. Dad suggested that I take her out later in the evenings, so I started taking her down there as dusk fell. She seemed more timid than ever and would stick so closely to me that it was difficult to move at all without tripping over her.

I did not insist on her investigating the holes, just tried to encourage her. I took her down to the huge set that had been there longer than any house in our village; it is mentioned in the Domesday Book, which was written in the eleventh century. Badgers are communal animals, and we hoped that Nikki's natural instinct would come to the fore and make her show some interest in animals of her own kind. But if anything, the reverse was true, and she was not settled again until a considerable distance had been put between the set and herself.

15

I HAD ONLY been home from school for a few minutes one Friday afternoon when the phone rang. I hurried to answer it, Nikki close to my heel as usual. It was a call for me. My friends from school often rang me up, and often I had to take phone messages for Mum or Dad, but this was the first telephone call for "Mr. St. John Burkett."

The man on the other end asked me if it was true that I had a badger that was allowed in the house and allowed its freedom. I told him that I had, and that it was sitting on my feet at that moment.

Nikki seemed to know that we were talking about her and tried to clamber up my legs, reaching out with a plump little paw toward the mouthpiece. Failing to achieve her objective, she occupied herself with the next best thing, which was the telephone wire. It took her about three seconds to get herself completely entangled. The telephone call developed into a wrestling match as I tried to retrieve enough of the wire to be able to carry on the conversation without having to lie on the floor.

The man introduced himself as a representative of Southern Television and wondered if we would allow him to take a film of the badger to show on television. I was delighted and excited. This was something to tell the boys! I had never met anyone who had actually been on television. The man must have sensed my excitement because he tried to water it down a bit. He said that he could not guarantee that they would *use* the film. He seemed eager enough to come up, though, and would have come that minute had the light been strong enough. However, we arranged for him to be up at the house at four o'clock on Monday afternoon.

I took my bike to school on Monday; the bus would not have got home quickly enough for me. I could not concentrate at all on the last class at school. I was home exactly two minutes after four, which was not bad going because it was nearly all uphill. There was no car outside the house, though. Mum said no one had come, and there had been no phone call either; she had been in all afternoon.

I waited beside the phone for an hour, but nothing happened. It was a real anticlimax. So I took Nikki and Tessa over the fields, and we did not come back until it was dark. The tawny owls were in full call, and I could see the barn owls hunting through the mist that was building up in the valley.

I was late home the next day, very late because I had

117

stopped to watch the football match. As soon as I turned the corner, I saw the car. There was no need to wonder whose it was, because there was a brightly colored sticker blazoned across the windscreen, saying, "Southern Television."

Somehow it did not mean so much now. I had been looking forward to his coming the day before, but it was not so exciting anymore. It had all fallen a bit flat.

Not for Nikki, though. She was entering fully into the spirit of the occasion. I found the photographer walking round the sitting room in laceless shoes, holding his camera above his shoulder in a peculiar way, presumably out of Nikki's reach. I gathered that he had been waiting for some time and was getting a bit impatient. Mum had not let him do any filming before I arrived.

I asked him why he had not come the previous day when we had expected him, and he said he had been out on another assignment. Mum told him that it was a pity he could not have let us know.

He told us exactly what he wanted: shots of the badger living with us in the house—the human angle, he called it. The first thing I had to do was go outside with Nikki and Tessa, then walk through the front door, across the hall, and upstairs, with them following. The photographer was enthusiastic about that shot and asked us to do it again. Then he decided that the light had not been quite right, so would we do it again. Seven times we repeated that sequence. Tessa gave up on the third. She sank onto the doormat with a great sigh and refused to budge an inch, which meant that I had to step over her and Nikki had to scramble over her each time.

Nikki was beginning to grow fractious after the last attempt. When the photographer suggested we come through the door yet again, I told him I thought Nikki had had more than enough of that particular exercise.

Next he wanted Mum and me and Sophie (who was home by this time) to sit at the table having our tea, while Nikki and Tessa ate from a bowl near us. I soon educated him on badger eating habits, explaining that Nikki was far more likely to want the food on the table than that on the floor. He did get some shots of the two animals eating from the same dish. The smell of food had made both of them splendidly cooperative in one second flat.

Sophie had changed into her best dress, and I suppose she did look pretty. Anyway, the cameraman seemed to think she was attractive and wanted her in the film. You could see Sophie was flattered. Anyway, he took some shots of Nikki trying to clamber up Sophie's legs and of her half-begging as Sophie held out a cookie. I say half-begging, for it could not have been called anything else. Nikki would sit up in the right position, but her weight seemed to be in all the wrong places, and she would always tumble over like one of those wobbly toys with a weighted base. Sophie rewarded her with tidbits, and the results seemed very satisfactory for both the photographer and the badger.

We had told him about some of Nikki's habits: how she hid our things and how she was intrigued by running water. The photographer decided he wanted shots of this, but you cannot turn an animal on and off like a tap, and Nikki was through cooperating. In any case, we had filled her up with tidbits. She climbed onto her armchair and lay on her back with her forepaws crossed on her bulging stomach, surveying the world through half-closed eyes.

The photographer went up to her and tried to make her move, and Nikki growled, a long deep growl which started at the base of the throat. The man drew back quickly.

I explained that the badger had had enough. She had been running round for over an hour and a half, and her patience was exhausted—not that she ever had much to start with. Patience is not a characteristic of badgers. I have watched one in the wild getting so angry with a twig that kept springing back across the path that he seized it in his mouth and shook it so vigorously that the whole plant came up.

I also explained to the photographer that you cannot get a general impression of an animal's behavior in such a short time. To get the kind of shots he was talking about, he would really need to come and sit with the family for at least a day, and we would be very pleased to help him.

But he did not seem eager to take up my offer. He said that he would see how the shots he already had would turn out. Sophie and I went out to the car to see him off.

I have never felt so flat in my life. The filming had not been nearly as exciting as I had expected. In fact, I thought it had all been rather boring, and I was sure the animals thought so too. I felt guilty at having subjected them to it and swore I would never do the same again.

Three days later the photographer phoned. The film had come out quite well, and they thought they could use it. They were going to show some of it the following Monday, and the producer would like to have Nikki in the studio. They would interview me with the animal as a follow-up to the film. I said yes, I would go, without giving it much thought.

It was lucky that Mum came in then. I quickly explained to her what it was all about, keeping my hand over the mouthpiece. She said she would like to know more about it and took the phone from my hand.

She was very short. She wanted to know what program I would be appearing on and what line the interviewer would be taking. She wanted to know why we would have to arrive at the studios so early if the program was not until the evening. Then I heard her say that there was no question of that, Nikki could not cope with more than one rehearsal. She finished by asking them to confirm the appointment in writing.

She did not seem very enthusiastic about the project.

Neither was my headmaster when I asked him if I could have the time off from school to go. I thought he would have been delighted. After all, there is an educational side to television. He explained that, officially, I should apply for a license from the education authorities, but as it was just an isolated occasion, he would give me permission this time.

Sophie was excited, of course. It does not take much to make Sophie excited.

I think Dad was, too. He was going to try to get the day off work so that he could come up with us. He also promised to buy me a new suit for the occasion. I would need one for the winter in any case, so we would get it that coming weekend.

16

THAT WEEKEND was the end of it all.

The whole family had gone to Winchester that afternoon to get my suit. I knew which one I wanted as soon as we went into the tailor's, but Mum did not like it. She thought it was far too tight and made me try on all sorts of old-fashioned styles. In the end we bought the one I had wanted from the beginning. I had a new shirt and tie as well. I let Mum choose those. After all, I had had my own way with the suit. I had new socks and shoes also.

Then we went into a café and had tea with cream cakes. We do not get out together very often, because we are generally so busy at home, so we made the most of this visit.

We sang all the way home. Dad taught us a song he had learned when he was in the service, and I think Mum was a bit shocked. She told Dad he ought to have known better, and that we did not need any encouraging. Then Tessa joined in. She put her head back and howled. I suppose she thought she was being musical.

We did not. Of course that made Sophie start to giggle, and you might as well give up when she starts giggling.

As soon as I opened the garden gate I knew something was terribly wrong.

The sight that met my eyes gave me such a shock that I could not move. I tried to make my feet go forward, but it was as if they were glued to the ground. I had to lean against the gatepost for support, and I felt sick, horribly, physically sick. The others seemed to come up behind me through a mist. Then I was jolted back into reality.

"Get them out," shouted Dad, in a tone that I had never heard before.

Sophie held open the gate, and Mum, Dad, and I rounded up the two yellow Labrador bitches that were careering round our garden. I thought one of them was going to turn on Dad. It faced him and bowed down low on its haunches, growling. Then they both turned and trotted unconcernedly down the hill. To this day we do not understand how they got in. We had a six-foot fence right round the garden which we considered completely dog-proof.

This particular pair of dogs had been a nuisance in the village for some time. They belonged to a couple who owned a cottage in the center of the village which they only used on weekends. Each weekend, as soon as they arrived, the dogs were let loose and allowed to run around the village leaving a trail of overturned trash cans behind them.

Overturned trash cans were the least we had to contend with that day. The door to the shed where we kept the sick birds was open, hanging loosely by one hinge. The interior of that shed was ominously silent. Dad got there first, and he shouted to Mum to get the heaters set up quickly. Two sparrowhawks were dead. They were just lying there. They showed no sign of injury, but they are nervous birds at the best of times, and the shock of the dogs must have been too much for them. One had come in with a broken wing, the other had been entangled in barbed wire. The ironic thing about the sparrowhawks was that they were both ready for release; if we had not gone out to get my suit that day, both of them would have been freed. There were five other birds in the shed, and although they seemed shocked, they recovered.

It was Nikki, though, that grieved us most.

I ran to her run. Thank goodness, those dogs had not been able to get in at her, although they had obviously tried, for the earth all round the run was dug up. And Nikki, my dear, affectionate, mischievous Nikki, was drawn up in one corner of the run, whimpering like a little baby—the way she had when we first saw her. It was a noise that went right to my heart, a noise I will never forget. I am certain now that it must have been dogs like these that got her from her set in the first place. She just huddled in that corner, shivering and terrified.

"Nikki, Nikki," I called, but she made no attempt

to answer me. She just sat there whimpering.

I opened the door of her run and reached in to get her. In that instant she moved. She made a mad dash at the door, diving through my legs. I put out my hands to stop her, but she slipped right through them. Out through her favorite hole in the hedge, across the field, and away.

I never saw her again.

I followed all our old familiar walks, calling, calling, calling her. Night after night I sat outside the badger sets, hoping that Nikki had found her way there. I would not have minded that. It was not knowing what

had happened to her that was so terrible. If only I could have caught a glimpse of her—if only I knew she was all right and was able to fend for herself—it would not have been so bad. Night after night I put out food for her in her run, just as I had always done.

It was never touched.

Tessa and I walked over and over the routes that the three of us had loved in those months of summer. I knew in my heart that it was hopeless but I had to go on looking.

Dad said that I would have to pull myself together, that Nikki was a wild animal, and that we had intended to let her go to the wild. We had never meant to keep her in captivity forever.

"I know," I cried, "but not like this. We wanted her to go in her own time. We didn't want her driven away."

I could not accept that I would never see Nikki again, or that the pain of her absence would ever let up—for her absence did hurt, really physically hurt. Every time I came home and no black and white tornado shot across the room toward me, it caused a pain in my chest that I could hardly bear.

Then one day, I just knew she was really gone.

That evening Tessa and I wandered over the fields. I stood and stared at the spot where Nikki had dug down the rabbit hole and got stuck. It had taken Dad and me until two o'clock in the morning to dig her out that time. I reached the old spot where I had so often sat while Nikki and Tessa ran and frisked in complete freedom and happiness, until the fat little badger came to squat on my feet, and Tessa lay down beside me with her mouth open and her tongue hanging out, her head cocked a little to one side.

Suddenly I missed Nikki so very much I could bear it no longer. I lay down on the damp grass and howled.

It was dark when I pulled myself together, dark and damp. I could see the lights of the traffic away on the main road, the noise dulled by the heavy autumn mist. As I sat up, dear old Tessa licked me down the side of my face as if she were saying, "I miss her too, you know."

As we returned home through the darkness, a home that had become so quiet and empty, I knew I would never forget that year. For me it would always be the year of the badger.